Worst Ideas Ever

A Celebration of Embarrassment

Daniel B. Kline AND **Jason Tomaszewski**

Skyhorse Publishing

Skyhorse Publishing books may be purchased in bulk at special discounts for sales promotion, corporate gifts, fund-raising, or educational purposes. Special editions can also be created to specifications. For details, contact the Special Sales Department, Skyhorse Publishing, 307 West 36th Street, 11th Floor, New York, NY 10018 or info@skyhorsepublishing.com.

Skyhorse® and Skyhorse Publishing® are registered trademarks of Skyhorse Publishing, Inc.®, a Delaware corporation.

www.skyhorsepublishing.com

10 9 8 7 6 5 4 3 2 1

Library of Congress Cataloging-in-Publication Data is available on file.
ISBN: 978-1-61608-262-8

Printed in China

To our wives, Celine Provini and Dawn Tomaszewski, for indulging our slow battle to become sort of famous. Some day we'll be bigger than Snooki and Bret Michaels put together and that is only possible with your support.

Contents

Introduction   1

FOOD & DRINK

New Coke   7

The Taco Bell Chihuahua   13

Alcoholic Energy Drinks   18

Edible Underwear   23

Deep-Frying a Turkey   26

Microwave Food   30

Death on a Plate   35

STUFF

The Segway   43

The Hindenburg   46

The Yugo   50

The Apple Newton   55

Atari Jaguar/Sega Dreamcast/Coleco Adam   58

The In-Car Phonograph   63

Laserdiscs   67

The Female Urinal   75

THE "ARTS"

Jar Jar Binks   81

Celebrity Albums   84

Adding a Cute Kid   87

CBS Radio Lets Howard Stern Go to Satellite   92

Jay Leno Moves to 10:00 PM   96

Battlefield Earth   103

Cop Rock   113

Godfather Part III   117

Theodore Rex   124

Worst TV Spin-Offs Ever   130

SPORTS

Michael Jordan Leaves Basketball for Baseball   139

Legendary Coach Jimmy Johnson Endorses
    Penis-Enhancement Pill   144

Major League Baseball Pushes the Sammy Sosa and Mark
   McGwire Home Run Chase   **151**

The XFL   **157**

Minnesota Vikings Trade Everything for Herschel Walker   **167**

Monday Night Football Hires Dennis Miller   **169**

The Trailblazers Choose Sam Bowie over Michael Jordan   **174**

The Bowl Champion Series   **178**

The LeBron James Decision   **183**

Disco Demolition Night   **189**

MEDIA & POLITICS

Politically Getting Ahead of Yourself   **198**

Stupid, Lying Politicians   **202**

AOL and Time Warner Merge   **208**

Esperanto   **213**

The Reebok Debacle   **219**

Prohibition   **221**

Celebrity Baby Names   **225**

Acknowledgements   **228**

Introduction

Bad ideas happen to everyone. We all wake up one morning and decide that we would look great in leather pants or that we can absolutely pull off those sunglasses we saw Elton John wearing. At some point, everyone not only has a bad idea, but they follow through on it. Whether it's telling your spouse you want to be in an open relationship or deciding "who needs a plumber, I can fix it myself," everyone has fallen victim to a bad idea.

A precious few, however, have been involved in a truly awful idea—an idea so bad that red flags should be flying while warning bells sound. These ideas—the worst ideas ever—stand out because anyone not involved in bringing them into being can simply look at the concept and know what an obvious disaster looms.

It's hard to imagine how some of these ideas come into existence and why nobody pointed out the obvious as everyone rushed headlong into disaster. Is it possible that nobody pulled Michael Jordan aside and said, "Baseball? You're the greatest basketball player ever, maybe you should stick with that."

Similarly, it's also fun to imagine the meeting where someone stood up in front of a roomful of Coke executives and said, "Eureka! I've got it. Why don't we get rid of our beloved product that outsells our rivals by huge amounts and completely change it?"

Any version of that meeting you can dream up ends in people laughing and suggesting that the person making the suggestion has had too much to drink. Instead, somebody must have said, "Good thinking, Pepsi would never expect that we would take our most popular product off the market. This strategy will really keep them guessing" or something of that ilk.

Whether it's the decision to put Whoopi Goldberg in a buddy cop movie where her buddy is a $35-million animatronic talking dinosaur or the one that involved putting record players in Chrysler cars, there are some bad ideas that simply transcend reality. For an idea to be one of the worst ideas ever, you have to consider the idea and not be able to imagine how someone—anyone—wouldn't talk the person out of it.

For example, after working for twelve straight hours getting this book ready to go, I turned to Jason and said, "What if we released the book only in Esperanto?" Since he had had a little more sleep, Jason was able to point out why our publisher might have issues with releasing a book in a failed language nobody speaks, not to mention the practical matter that neither of us speaks it. You wonder where someone like Jason was when Vince McMahon pitched the XFL or when Stephen Bochco stood in front of ABC executives and told them about *Cop Rock*, a police procedural/Broadway musical that actually made it on the air.

Bad ideas are like bad haircuts as the damage fades with time. Nobody teases me about my pink skinny tie from junior high, and my friends rarely bring up the period when I decided that I should sport Pat Riley's hairstyle. Similarly, I only occasionally still tease Jason about his days wearing the Michael Jackson single glove, and our buddies rarely bring up the period he carried a purse (he still insists it was a "man bag," which, frankly, sounds worse than purse).

If you're the guy that green-lit *Battlefield Earth* or are the person at Apple who pushed the Newton through, well, I doubt you get off that easy.

Daniel Kline

FOOD & DRINK

New Coke—Replacing the Market-Leading Product with One People Hate

Up until 1985, the formula for Coca-Cola had remained unchanged for ninety-nine years. During that time, the beverage had become the clear market leader, widely outpacing rival Pepsi in sales and becoming an iconic brand whose logo was recognizable from Tehran to Tahiti. So of course, troubled by this unparalleled success, the executives in charge of the Coca-Cola empire decided to change the formula, making it sweeter and more like its less-successful competitor.

Introduced on April 23, 1985, "New Coke" sparked an immediate consumer outrage. While Coca-Cola executives claimed they had introduced the new product to "reenergize the brand," the move had the opposite effect: leaving customers feeling betrayed and angry. Basically, the company had taken a drink beloved by millions—partially because it was an American classic that never changed—and changed it just to shake things up.

The original announcement of the change actually led to die-hard Coke fanatics buying and stockpiling large quantities of the beverage and storing it to drink after the new product was introduced. Actual protest groups including "Society for the Preservation of the Real Thing" popped up, and Coca-Cola's 1-800-GET-COKE line was flooded with complaints.

Anger at New Coke was so strong that the company was forced to bring back the original formula a mere seventy-nine days later on July 11, 1985. The revived original brand dubbed "Coca-Cola Classic" was sold alongside its much less popular, doomed replacement for a few years, with Coca-Cola attempting to market New Coke to younger audiences who presumably enjoyed sweeter beverages. Eventually, New Coke was renamed "Coke II" before it was taken off the market in the United States—though it continues to be sold in some foreign countries.

The swiftness with which Coca-Cola reintroduced its original formula has led to much speculation that the entire New Coke introduction was merely a marketing ploy to get people excited about the brand again. Though marketing personnel at the company probably wish that had been the case, Coke's executives have always denied that there had been any plan, insisting that they were actually dumb enough to decide to change what wasn't broken.

Worst Soda Spin-Offs Ever

- **Crystal Pepsi.** The makers of Pepsi were so sure that their clear cola product would be the next big thing that they spent millions of dollars licensing Van Halen's hit, "Right Now," for its launch campaign. Though ads blanketed the country and many people likely sampled the beverage after its 1992 introduction, few liked it, and it disappeared from shelves before the end of 1993.

- **Seven Up Gold.** This product mixed 7Up's vaguely lemon-lime formula with cinnamon, resulting in a sewage-brown soft drink that vanished from stores so quickly that many today still doubt its existence.

- **Pepsi Blue.** Introduced in 2002, PepsiCo's Web site described this product as a fusion of berries with a splash of cola and claimed the blue-hued soft drink was created by and for teens. Teens, apparently, didn't like their own creation—seeing as it is no longer sold.

- **Pepsi Kona:** Surprisingly, the people at Pepsi are responsible for an awful lot of truly terrible beverages. This one was a coffee-flavored beverage that was hyper-caffeinated. In some ways, this was the grandfather of the energy drink craze as Pepsi was truly ahead of its time in creating a highly caffeinated drink that tastes awful.

- **The Jones Soda Holiday Pack.** The Jones company has gotten a lot of publicity over creating wacky flavors that nobody wants. Still, however, there's a difference between making key lime pie soda as a publicity stunt and unleashing these monstrosities on the drinking public. The holiday pack included the following flavors: Brussels Sprout with Prosciutto, Cranberry Sauce, Wild Herb Stuffing, Broccoli Casserole, Smoked Salmon Paté, Turkey & Gravy and Corn on the Cob.

The Taco Bell Chihuahua: "Dogs Just Love Our Food."

Sometimes fame does not accurately measure success. That can certainly be considered the case for Gidget, the Taco Bell Chihuahua. Perhaps the most famous pitch-dog since "the original party dog" Spuds McKenzie, the Taco Bell Chihuahua appeared in a very popular series of commercials for the low-priced taco chain. As these ads ran, the dog became a legitimate celebrity. Toy figures were made. The Chihuahua appeared on TV, shirts, and well, if a dog can be star, this one certainly was.

Much like Clara Peller and her famous "Where's the beef?" catchphrase, the Taco Bell Chihuahua first achieved stardom for its trademark saying, "Yo quiero Taco Bell." This line also appeared on T-shirts and became one of the more ripped-off advertising slogans. Much like the way versions of *What happens in Vegas stays in Vegas* got turned into "What happens at Marty Goldstein's Bar Mitzvah stays at Marty Goldstein's Bar Mitzvah," the "Yo quiero" line was everywhere in every ridiculous form possible.

The dog also managed to briefly make the line "Drop the chalupa!" popular when, for some reason, that particular phrase was briefly picked up by various SportsCenter anchors. Still, all this notoriety seems like a positive thing, as the Chihuahua certainly raised Taco Bell's brand awareness. Unfortunately, while the dog was famous and more people knew about Taco Bell, less people actually ate there. A talking dog who loves your restaurant's food, it seems, while cute, does not exactly send the right message to the public. Instead, it apparently sent the message, "Our food is dog food," and despite the wildly popular (and expensive) ad campaigns, sales actually slumped for the chain.

Perhaps more importantly, Taco Bell not only decided to use a dog in its commercials, the chain decided to use a dog typically associated with Mexican people. Though Taco Bell sells Mexican food, choosing a Chihuahua as its representative seemed more than a little like stereotyping—a fact not unnoticed by the Hispanic community. This was not helped by the fact that the dog was often depicted as a Mexican revolutionary wearing a beret or as a bandido wearing a sombrero. Taco Bell stopped short of dressing the dog as a maid or as day laborer, but the damage was done, and ultimately, the commercials were pulled due to pressure from Hispanic groups.

To make matters worse, in 2003 Taco Bell lost a lawsuit brought forth by two Michigan men who had pitched the concept of the Chihuahua to Taco Bell six years earlier. Taco Bell had turned them down but went forward with the campaign with its advertising agency, TBWA. A jury awarded the two men $30.1 million in compensation plus nearly $12 million in additional interest. To get its money back, Taco Bell sued TBWA, claiming that the agency should have been aware of the conflicts. In 2009 a three-judge federal appeals panel ruled against Taco Bell.

Gidget was put to sleep on July 21, 2009, after having a stroke in the home of her trainer. The globally famous dog and beloved spokesperson was cremated, and her ashes were retained by her trainer.

The Noid

A media sensation like the Taco Bell Chihuhua, the Noid was an evil character with rabbit ears in a red suit who constantly attempted to ruin Domino's Pizza. The commercials used the catchphrase "Avoid the Noid," and there was even an "Avoid the Noid" video game spin-off based on the character. Of course, the Noid was constantly thwarted in his attempts to ruin the Domino's pizza.

The problem here is, of course, that no cartoon character was needed in the 1980s to ruin a Domino's pizza. People ate Domino's because it was convenient (they delivered) and quick (it was free if they took more than half an hour) so the minimum wage delivery people regularly risked their lives getting it to you. Nobody ate Domino's because it was good pizza. The only way the Noid could ruin a Domino's Pizza would be if somehow he added even crummier ingredients, which would be hard as Domino's Pizza tasted like it was ketchup smeared on a cardboard box. Domino's even acknowledged that fact in a series of commercials that began in 2010 that acknowledged that its pizza was terrible.

3

Alcoholic Energy Drinks: You'll Have No Idea How Drunk You Are

Though most people think of alcohol as being something that makes them feel good, it's actually a depressant. A few beers or a couple of belts of whiskey might relax you, causing you to let down your guard and enjoy the party a bit (or maybe a lot) more, but booze is actually a major downer. In addition to lowering inhibitions, a few drinks will also slow down your reactions, impair your vision and generally make you sleepy. So, while you're dancing at that party with a lampshade on your head, you're actually in a depressed state and that effect is what actually stops most normal people from drinking to excess. Either we get sleepy and leave the bar or if we're imbibing a little too much we pass out (and hopefully a friend rolls us on our side).

Energy drinks have exactly the opposite effect. These beverages—like Monster, Red Bull, Venom, Krunk!!! and many others—contain a lot of sugar and a whole lot of caffeine. Most energy drinks have way more caffeine than a similar-sized coffee and people tend to drink energy drinks in much bigger containers than your typical cup of coffee. Used properly, energy drinks are a way to pep yourself up in the morning or during a long night of studying. Used in excess, energy drinks can make you twitchy, paranoid, and somewhat immune to sleep.

Both alcohol and energy drinks have their uses, but the real problems started occurring when people began combining the two products. This first happened at bars and in private homes where people began quaffing the popular combination of Red Bull and vodka. This led to companies beginning to market colorful cans of energy/alcoholic drinks which looked an awful lot like their non-alcoholic counterparts (which made it that much easier for the underage to buy these beverages which, of course, never occurred to any of the marketing people behind the products).

And, while both alcohol and energy drinks can cause problems on their own, when joined together, the results can be truly horrible. Alcohol makes you sleepy and energy drinks keep you up. Combine the two and you get a drunk guy who has no idea he's drunk. The caffeine and sugar in the energy drink masks the drowsying effect of the alcohol and though you're getting drunker, you feel more awake then ever, making it possible to drink even more alcoholic energy drinks. As the drinker downs more and more of these adult beverages, he feels less drunk, which can lead to not doing the things drunks normally do like pass out or stop drinking. Instead, since he doesn't feel drunk, the drinker thinks he's okay to drive or that it's a great idea to call up his ex-wife and tell her how he really feels about her.

With alcoholic energy drinks you can stay up drinking all night long as the caffeine will keep you going while the booze tries to slow you down. This works out great if you're an alcoholic musician or a stand-up comedian working the late show. For regular people, drinking endlessly and never feeling you're all that drunk tends to sometimes lead to hilarious stories (and when I woke up, I had no idea what her name was) and, more often than not, really bad ones (no officer, I don't remember strangling that hooker).

As alcoholic energy drinks moved from the bar to the liquor store, even more problems arose as most of these upper/downer concoctions were packaged in cans. Generally, they looked like double-sized beers, leading the teenagers and college kids who gravitated towards these products to assume that the cans would be roughly the equivalent of drinking a beer. If the young booze-hound could drink a 12-pack of beer on a normal friday night, he would, of course, assume he could down at least half a dozen of these alcoholic energy drinks.

Unfortunately, most alcoholic energy drinks packaged to look like double-sized beers actually contain the alcohol content of four to five beers. That means that the kid who thinks he's having four beers might actually be having ten. This has, of course, led to deaths (from alcohol poisoning) and murders (in Connecticut one guy stabbed his girlfriend to death after drinking just two of these).

Edible Underwear: Finally, Romance Gets Sticky?

While one can see the romantic logic for edible undergarments, the actual execution pointed out some obvious flaws. In theory, one would wear these as a romantic gift for a significant other who would devour them in a fit of passion.

The problems arose when one considered what it actually took to make edible underwear (which really should have been called edible panties because if a male version existed, it was not well-marketed). The underwear was basically made of a thin version of the material that goes into a Fruit Roll-Up. This gelatinous sugary goo was shaped into underwear shapes in a variety of sizes and styles and, of course, flavors.

Unfortunately, as anyone who has ever eaten a Fruit Roll-Up knows, that particular material does not respond well to handling or warmth. Sticky in the first place, a Fruit Roll-Up becomes quite horrible to handle when combined with any sort of warmth or moisture. That's fine when it happens in a small, rolled-up fruit snack you handle with your hands. It becomes more of a problem when the "snack" is covering your nether regions.

Unless you sat entirely still in a chilled room, the idea of putting on edible underwear as a surprise to your partner results in utter disaster as the candy quickly melts and sticks you to the unlucky lady's body. And, of course, when this product had its heyday in the mid 1970s through the 1980s, women were, for the most part, hairier in their bikini zone (as the TV commercials for hair removal products refer to that area), resulting in not only a sticky mess, but a painful sticky mess as removing the underwear involved ripping out the hair to which it would become stuck.

Even if the edible panties did not melt before a lady's partner got the chance to devour them, the product was still a failure as eating a pair of sticky underwear off your partner's nether regions was a better-sounding proposition than a reality. After a few bites, the saliva from the eater's mouth eventually produced the same sticky effect, usually curtailing any romantic activity and instead leading to a frantic effort to remove the supposedly romantic edible underthings without hurting the person wearing them or soiling the bed sheets with melted candy underwear.

Edible underwear exists to this day and can be purchased in novelty shops and sex stores, but the idea has dramatically faded in popularity moving the product more from "romantic idea" to "novelty gift" where people give them but nobody actually uses them.

Deep-Frying a Turkey: Bring a Bomb to Your House or Backyard

Nearly anything can be deep-fried. You can put any manner of meat, fish, vegetable, and even candy bars into a deep fryer. At fairs and festivals around the country, people deep-fry Twinkies, pizza, and even Coke syrup. There are entire restaurants devoted to frying odd things, which people are more than willing to do. Some shops even let you bring in your own stuff to fry, so if you have allergies and want a deep-fried Claritin, well, they might do that for you.

Frying at home, however, can be a dangerous proposition. Nearly everyone who has ever attempted to cook with oil—even if it's just a small amount on a stovetop—has, at some point, burned themselves in the splatter. Deep fryers can be dangerous too, and anyone who has worked at a fast food place—even with their regimented safety measures—usually ends up with burns on his arms, fingers, and hands. Dipping uncooked food in burning oil is dangerous in a controlled situation (like a restaurant), but it can be downright deadly when people attempt to do it in their backyard or even inside their house.

The perils of deep-frying a turkey begin with the fact that most things that go into a deep fryer or a Fryolator are relatively small. French fries, pieces of chicken (not whole chickens), and anything in nugget form work well in a deep fryer. Nobody tries to make a friend roast beef or a fried leg of lamb (or if they did, they did not survive the process). There's a reason for that as deep fryers cook from the outside in, and they cook very quickly. Cook something big in a deep fryer and you run the risk of charring the outside while the inside remains raw.

So the initial danger of cooking a turkey this way is that you will ruin the outer layers of meat while the inner ones remain underdone. This could lead to all sorts of types of food poisoning, which while probably very authentic on Thanksgiving, does not make for a pleasant family get-together.

The second major danger of cooking a large bird in a deep fryer is that it will blow up, likely maiming the chef, anyone standing near the chef, and perhaps, burning the house down.

This happens because you cannot deep-fry a turkey in a normal home deep fryer. To do that, you would have to cut the turkey up into smaller pieces, and nobody comes to Thanksgiving hoping for a chunk of turkey. Instead, turkeys must be deep fried in a dedicated turkey deep fryer. These are essentially electric barrels, which heat the oil to an unholy temperature, into which the cook must somehow figure out how to drop a turkey without splashing molten-lava-temperature oil on himself.

In addition to the dangers of food poisoning and oil splashing, there is the imminent danger that the entire apparatus might catch fire and explode. This can happen in a number of fun and exciting ways. Turkey deep fryers are usually shaped like a canister trash can. That makes them relatively easy to tip over, which spills hot oil over your house, yard, or deck, likely causing a fire. Further compounding this problem is that turkey deep fryers are usually propane-powered. A fire near a source of propane results in a fairly powerful bomb that can take out a pretty big section of a house.

Underwriters Laboratory (UL) is an organization that essentially certifies which products are safe and which ones aren't. UL does not certify any turkey deep fryer because they do not deem that any of the many on the market are actually safe to use.

"There are no UL listed turkey fryers because the turkey fryers on the market do not have the level of safety features we deem necessary," said John Drengenberg, a spokesman for UL to the *New York Times* on Nov. 25, 2008. "Most turkey fryers are essentially a large pot over sitting on a frame over an open propane flame," he explained. "Most don't have thermostat controls, and there are situations when the hot oil can spill over into the fire. Then you've got something like a vertical flame thrower in your hands."

Even more turkey fryers explode when they are either over-filled with oil or when a partially frozen turkey gets placed in the oil. The water from the ice in the partially frozen turkey can literally result in an effect that basically turns your fryer into a flamethrower.

6

Microwave Food: Maybe a Shake Does Not Need to Be Microwaved?

Microwaves make sense for heating up water for tea, reheating certain leftovers, and warming up dinner if it has been out of the oven or off the stove for too long. Even certain prepackaged microwave meals like Lean Cuisines are not entirely awful, but when the microwave first became popular, people were eager to cook anything and everything in the device. You could buy pans to make roasts in your microwaves (which resulted in roasts with the consistency of

leather boots) and special devices to cook everything from pota-
toes to bacon.

In the 1980s, as microwaves became popular and a fixture
in nearly every home (the ones with dial-based timers and doors
that might open without turning off the microwaves), companies began releasing pretty much any food you can think of in
microwaveable form. Some of the more ridiculous ones included
the microwave shake—which was essentially a frozen-solid block
of shakelike chemicals that you melted in your microwave. The
resulting sludge neither looked like nor tasted like an actual
shake. It was more like hot ice cream soup with frozen chunks
floating in it. No setting or amount of time in the microwave
produced the correct texture.

Another popular microwave product that never should have
been made was the microwave cake. This came in both mix form

and premade in microwaveable pans. In either case, the resulting product that emerged from the microwave looked like cake. But while it looked like a cake, it tasted more like a Nerf football. Cake should, theoretically, be moist and maybe a bit crumbly. Microwave cake had the consistency of the old Styrofoam containers McDonald's used to sell everything in.

Perhaps the worst microwave product ever, though, was the microwave hamburger. Though there were various companies that released microwave burgers, all of them had the same basic premise. It was an entire burger/bun combo (sometimes with condiments) that got heated up in a microwaveable sleeve. These sleeves (which were also included with the microwave Belgian waffles) had metal on the inside, which seemed like a bad idea as everyone knows that putting metal in a microwave results in a veritable lightning storm inside your microwave. Somehow, the cardboard sleeve acted as a shield for the metal, which magically then cooked your burger. Of course, it cooked your burger, so half of it was ice cold and the other half was molten lava hot. That didn't really matter though because the consistency of the burger was so wrong that it was difficult to tell where the bun ended and the burger began.

One of the key problems with microwave burgers, shakes, cakes, and other items was that it was not significantly quicker or easier to make them in the microwave. The reason someone would, say, boil water for tea in the microwave and not put a kettle on the stove is that the microwave does in just over a minute what takes six to eight minutes on the stove. With products like burgers, cakes, and shakes, that was not really true because any time saved was spent putting your food back into the microwave, trying to get a consistent temperature.

Death on a Plate: The Krispy Kreme Burger

Americans are always looking for new ways to kill ourselves. From extreme sports to competitive eating, we are eager to test the edges of human endurance even when no particular reason to do so exists. This has led to us attempting to fry nearly everything possible (fried pizza seems a bit excessive) and to creative cooks finding ways to combine foods that don't actually go together. Perhaps the worse of these would be the Krispy Kreme burger.

For the uninitiated, Kripsy Kremes are extremely addictive donuts that are made on a conveyor belt and served fresh. Few people eat just one of these calorie bombs and in many cases—if the donuts are coming off the conveyor belt hot—a Krispy Kreme employee will actually hand you a fresh donut as soon as you step into the store while you consider what to order. The donut is merely an appetizer to the actual meal which will consist of more donuts, because that's really the only thing on the menu at a Krispy Kreme.

Hamburgers are, of course, a staple of the American diet. Not exactly health food, burgers consist of ground beef and various toppings served on a bun. Both the Krispy Kreme and the hamburger are delicious, but neither could be considered good for you and both pack a lot of calories. One is, of course, a sweet treat, while the other would have to be considered savory. The only reason one could think of to mix the two products would be the fact that donuts are sort of shaped like a hamburger bun. Otherwise, a donut-burger makes about as much sense as pouring beef gravy over a slice of chocolate cake.

That complete lack of compatibility did not, however, stop one minor league baseball team from creating a combination Krispy Kreme/hamburger. This death-defying treat was introduced as a publicity stunt. That would be just fine if the public—ever eager to die quicker—didn't jump on the bandwagon and actually start eating the things.

The burger features a Black Angus all-beef patty covered in melted cheese and two strips of bacon served between a sliced, deep-fried Krispy Kreme donut. On the plus side, at least the Gateway Grizzlies, a team in the Illinois' Frontier League that serves the treat (which was created in Atlanta), resisted the urge to use two separate donuts as the bun. Still, the Krispy Kreme burger packs more than 1,000 calories and enough saturated fat to give an Olympic athlete a heart attack.

The KFC Double Down

Kentucky Fried Chicken once was so worried about its reputation as a purveyor of unhealthy treats that the chain actually attempted to rebrand itself as KFC. Of course, they still sold almost entirely fried chicken, but by dropping the name, they at least created the appearance of trying to be healthier. For a while, the newly rechristened KFC actually pushed its grilled chicken option in an attempt to court customers seeking healthier alternatives.

All that effort went for naught, however, when KFC introduced the Double Down, this monstrosity decided that the bun was just a waste of space. So, instead of some bread, the Double Down used two fried chicken patties as the outside of the sandwich. Served in a grease-saturated cardboard sleeve, the Double Down features the aforementioned two fried chicken breasts, bacon, cheese and special sauce. KFC claims this "treat" only contains 540 calories, but a number of websites dispute that total. Either way, eating two fried chicken breasts, two slices of cheese and two pieces bacon all slathered in special sauce is a recipe for heading to an early grave.

STUFF

8

The Segway:
Two Wheels
and a Dream

Looking like the illegitimate child of hand truck and a unicycle, the Segway was supposed to revolutionize how people got around. These two-wheeled, self-balancing personal transports were touted as the next great invention—something that would change the way people live their lives, Instead, the Segway turned into a novelty that people might rent while on a vacation, the land-based equivalent of one of those boats you propel by pedaling.

Invented by supposed genius Dean Kamen (if your type of genius invents stuff nobody actually buys), the Segway uses a very clever system of gyroscopic sensors to stay balanced. The rider actually stands up on the machine, telling it which way to go by shifting his weight about. The driver uses the handlebars to turn and, in optimal circumstances, Segways can go up to 12.5 miles per hour.

A clever concept, the problems begin for Segway when one begins to consider practical uses. Let's pretend that someone living in a city like New York was legally allowed to use the Segway as transportation (you aren't). Exactly how many places do people go where they only need to transport themselves? The Segway's design does not exactly allow for luggage and major cities do not have a lot of places to safely store this type of device. So, that makes the Segway perfect for short trips where you won't need anything with you other than what you can carry and where you can either lock your vehicle up somewhere or not mind too much when it gets stolen.

The second major problem with Segway is that despite its supposed safety and ease-of-use, the average driver has a bit of a learning curve. It's possible to fall off of a Segway and it's possible to drive your Segway into things. Driving while standing up is not a natural position to most people who generally learn to drive while sitting in a car.

Segways, like any other vehicle, can also be driven places they should not go—a problem magnified by the fact that not every driver instantly picks up how to safely use the vehicle. This problem came to the forefront when Jim Heselden—the owner of Segway—accidently drove his off a cliff, leading to his death. In general, when the owner of your company accidently kills himself while attempting to use your product, it's hard to consider that good publicity.

Still, despite its occasional ability to cause the death of its driver (realistically that can be said of any vehicle) the Segway's biggest fault comes in the fact that in most of the places you would want to use one, they are not legal to drive. Since no cities have Segway lanes and a vehicle which is essentially a stand-up bicycle is not safe for the streets, this leaves Segway riders to the sidewalks. In many places this is actually outlawed and in other it is simply not well-tolerated by actual pedestrians.

This has left the Segway as a fairly innovative product with no constituency. A few police departments have put Segway into limited use but, let's face it, the only thing less intimidating than a police officer on a bike is one driving a Segway. Mostly, Segways have been reduced to novelty vehicles that you can rent at various tourist destinations—like a less fun jet ski or motorcycle that goes slower than a fast bicycle.

The Hindenburg: People Plus a Balloon Filled with Gas and Oxygen Equals Disaster

Before airplanes were a viable method of moving groups of people around, blimps (called airships at the time) were considered a reasonable way to travel. Airships were not particularly efficient vehicles and even in their heyday, only the very wealthy could afford to use them. The Hindenburg was a large airship that could carry seventy passengers, but to do that, the blimp required approximately forty crew members.

Airships were essentially long, stretched-out versions of what we now call a hot air balloon. Instead of the balloon shape, the airship looked more like a football, and instead of the basket there was an enclosed passenger cabin. Unlike today's blimps, which are essentially balloons, the huge Zeppelin

transoceanic models like the Hindenburg actually had a rigid full skeleton supporting the balloon. The ship was steered with a mix of rudders and propellers. The size of a cruise ship (only eighty or so feet smaller than the *Titanic*), the Hindenburg remains the largest vehicle to ever fly, and before its horrifying end, it was meant to be the first of a huge fleet.

The problem comes when you consider exactly how an airship like the Hindenburg stayed in the air. Basically, the Hindenburg was a giant balloon filled with hydrogen, and like any balloon, it was susceptible to popping. More importantly, in this case, the airship was a huge balloon made of flammable materials filled with hydrogen, which is also flammable. Then chairman of the company that built the Hindenburg, Zeppelin, Dr. Hugo Eckener actually had initially decided that the airship should be inflated with nonflammable helium.

Unfortunately, that was impossible because Zeppelin, having undergone some tough financial times, had accepted money from Germany's Nazi party. The Hindenburg and its sister ship, Graf Zeppelin, were adorned with Swastikas as they were both flown on a variety of propaganda flights over Germany. This made it impossible to obtain the necessary helium required for the vessel as the only suitable natural deposits of helium in the world were in the United States. Though the United States was not at war with Germany quite yet, more than a few Americans were not exactly trusting of Adolph Hitler, and Congress passed the "Helium Control Act," which made exporting the gas illegal. So that basically left the Hindenburg as a giant flying bag of flammable gas housed in a flammable casing.

All it would take was one spark to set the Hindenburg ablaze, and because of that, all lighters and matches were confiscated from passengers. Of course, since these were rich people and smoking was still allowed on board in a special asbestos-lined smoking room, a convenient built-in lighter was provided in the passenger cabin.

If you fill a giant bag with flammable gas and then allow people to smoke on board, it's hard to imagine that something horrible won't happen. Still, the Hindenburg had made numerous successful flights—which seems hard to imagine—before its fateful journey.

The actual disaster—made famous because of the incredible news footage shot and the "Oh, the humanity" line uttered by a reporter—took place took place on Thursday, May 6, 1937, as the Hindenburg caught fire and was destroyed during its attempt to dock at the Lakehurst Naval Air Station in Lakehust, New Jersey.

The ship was only carrying half its full capacity of passengers (thirty-six of seventy seats were filled), but it had an extra complement of trainee crew members and so there were sixty-one crew aboard. Of the ninety-seven people aboard, thirty-five died as did one person on the ground. The actual cause of the fire remains unknown, although a variety of theories have been suggested over the years.

Of course, exactly how the Hindenburg caught fire was irrelevant as a giant balloon filled with flammable gas was bound the eventually go up in flames. After the Hindenburg disaster, travel via airship fell out of favor, and now, blimps are only used for sporting events and advertising, and, of course, they are filled with nonflammable helium.

The Yugo:
Finally, a
Disposable Car

In Europe and Asia, poorly made tiny cars are not entirely uncommon as many countries lack the basic safety standards we have in the United States. In parts of the world, seatbelts are not mandatory, and making sure a car does not crumple into pieces upon impact might be less important than saving a few dollars.

The Yugo, however, took these low standards and brought them to the United States where, while we had seen lousy cars before (the Gremlin), we had never seen anything quite this inferior. Yugos were light, cheap, and they fell apart if you leaned on them. The first Yugos were one model available in red, white, and blue—perhaps to create the idea that this vehicle named after a war-torn country that most Americans had never heard of and would soon dissolve were, in fact, as American as apple pie, mom, and country music. On the positive side, the car was cheap (about $4,500 in 1984) and it came with a ten-year/hundred-thousand-mile warranty—figures rendered irrelevant by the fact that no Yugo ever made it anywhere near either of those numbers without crumpling into dust.

At first, five models of Yugo were sold in the United States: the basic entry-level $3,990 GV (for "Great Value"), the GVC

with a glass sunroof, the nearly identical GVL and GVS with minor trim and upholstery upgrades, and the race-inspired GVX with the 1,300 cc engine, five-speed manual transmission and standard equipment including a plush interior, ground-effects package, alloy wheels, rally lights and more. A "Cabrio" convertible was introduced in 1988, and somehow, likely due to price, the brand gained a small foothold in the United States, all the while building up a reputation for not being reliable and falling apart quickly. Reviewers often explained that it was a much better deal to buy a used car costing the same as a new Yugo, but some were simply suckered in by the allure of owning a brand-new car even if that car was legendarily a piece of junk.

The bottom fell out for Yugo when, in 1990, the company attempted to introduce an electronic fuel injection (EFI) model. Sadly, that happened a little too late as the company was already being investigated for failing to meet U.S. emission standards. This led to the recall of over 126,000 Yugos sold in the United States—that's every Yugo sold to that point in the country. Ultimately, that caused Yugo to end its U.S. operations in 1992.

As the company was failing in the United States, it was also failing around the world. By the early 1990s, the United Nations had specifically sanctioned the company, forcing it to withdraw its products from every export market. Eventually, the company was destroyed for good when NATO forces bombed its parent companies' auto division instead of its arms production facility.

Still, as late as the mid 2000s, there was talk of reviving the brand and bringing it back to the United States, perhaps with a name change as Yugoslavia no longer exists.

Le Car

Briefly marketed in the United States, the Le Car was actually a popular model in Europe for French automaker Renault. In Europe, it was known as the Renault 5, and some of the things that made it an oddball in the U.S. market (such as the tiny engine that allowed the spare tire to be kept under the front seat) made it popular in Europe. In the United States, however, the car was given the Le Car name, and while it may have been ahead of its time as a compact, fuel-efficient car, its effeminate look and the silly name made it essentially a novelty product bought only by hipsters and Francophiles.

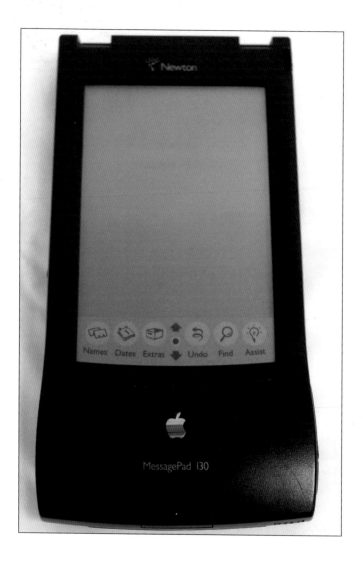

11

The Apple Newton: What if a Rolodex Mixed with a Calendar Cost $699?

Some would say that the eventual rampant success of other personal digital assistants (PDA) ultimately validates the Apple Newton as a good idea. That, however, would be like calling a caveman who glues feathers to his body and attempts to fly a visionary because, ultimately, someone invented the airplane.

Similarly, it could be forgiven if the Newton had failed in only one area. If it had been a perfect product except for its often-mocked handwriting recognition, then it would go down as an idea ahead of its time instead of as the unmitigated disaster that almost sunk Apple.

Instead, the Newton failed on numerous levels. First, it was the size of a hardcover book, weighed nearly a pound, and was at best impractical as a "portable" device. It also cost $699 upon its 1993 launch, making it unaffordable to Apple's then target audience of students, journalists, and tech hipsters. It also included a nonbacklit LCD screen with poor contrast that made reading difficult in good conditions and nearly impossible with any sort of sunlight.

When the Newton was put into development in 1987, cell phones did not exist in any practical form. When it was released in August of 1993, technology had advanced, but laptops were still the size of small suitcases, and cell phones were reserved for top executives and rich kids looking to impress girls.

Apple executives did not want the Newton to compete with their Macintosh computers, so the device was specifically given limited functionality. Instead of being a handheld computer that would justify its price tag, the Newton was essentially a heavy address book where entering names was quite the challenge.

Theoretically, the Newton had handwriting recognition software that allowed it to learn a user's writing and adapt to get the letters correct. As you wrote on the touch screen with the included stylus, it was supposed to get better and better at interpreting your writing, eventually making entering data as simple as writing on the screen.

In reality, the handwriting recognition never worked and simply guessed at letters. Try to enter "Call Tony at 4PM" and you could easily get "Kill Pony at farm"—good for comedy, but not that useful as a personal assistant. The poor handwriting recognition provided fodder for late-night comedians to mock the product and even got parodied on a *Simpsons'* episode when "Ha Ha" bully Nelson Muntz wrote "Beat up Martin" on his Newton only to have it recognize the words as "Eat up Martha."

A pretty much immediate failure, Apple, unused to failing, clung to the device for a number of years. Before it was ultimately killed in February of 1998, Apple spun off the Newton into its own company, Newton Inc., but that company was reabsorbed several months later when Steve Jobs ousted Apple CEO Gil Amelio and resumed control of Apple.

Atari Jaguar/ Sega Dreamcast/ Coleco Adam: The Game Systems Nobody Wanted

t various times, Atari, Sega, and Coleco all ruled the video game console world, having essentially all of the business. Similarly, all three companies would follow up their market-leading consoles with horrible systems that not only knocked themselves out of the top spot, but literally put their companies (well two of the three) entirely out of business.

When Atari released the 2600 in 1977, it actually did not in any way revolutionize the video game universe. That wouldn't happen until 1982 when games like Space Invaders and later

Pac-Man became available for the console. Sold with two simple one-button joysticks and a second set of paddle controls, Atari was essentially the first home video game console. While there had been others, they were basically just machines that came with a few built-in games—all of which were variants of Pong.

Atari ruled this new category for years, selling over eight million units in 1982 alone as well as millions of cartridges. Atari, to most people, was the entire home video game industry, and the only way the company could lose its market dominance would be to completely botch the release of its next generation.

Though the Atari 2600 had a remarkable life span, its lack of processing power and games that were vastly inferior to what could be found in arcades eventually made it necessary for Atari to release an updated version. Enter the Jaguar, Atari's 1993 attempt at replacing the 2600. The first problem with the Jaguar was that in its attempt to milk every last dime of revenue out of the 2600 market, Atari had simply waited too long. Though Atari had released a variety of updates to the 2600, it had largely been surpassed by the Nintendo Entertainment System (NES) and its Super Mario Brothers game. Though the NES's graphics seem laughable now, they were light-years ahead of the 2600.

The Jaguar was supposed to be the answer to that, but by the time it was released, the battle had already been lost. Not only had Nintendo become the number one name in videogames, essentially by default, but that company was actually already releasing its next-generation system (the not-that-successful Super Nintendo Entertainment System) and the Sega Genesis had emerged and was beginning a rise in popularity that would ultimately place Sega at the top of the console heap for a while.

During its heyday, the Atari 2600 faced a number of competitors, including Intellivison (which branded itself as "Intelligent Television" as its keypad had a lot of numbers), which led to un-fun games where you pressed numeric combinations to do things and the highly regarded ColecoVision. Superior to the 2600 and in-line with the 2600, ColecoVision made its parent company, Coleco, a player in the market for a brief moment before they too botched their chance at a follow-up by launching the Coleco Adam, a sort of cross between a videogame player and early home computers like the Commodore 64. The Adam, though, was neither a good video game console nor a very useful home computer.

It failed miserably partly because it was a poorly conceived product and partly because of glitches like the fact that it generated a surge of electromagnetic energy on startup, which often erased the contents of any removable media left in or near the drive. This problem was compounded by the fact that some of the Coleco manuals instructed the user to put the tape in the drive before turning the computer on, basically telling the gamers to do the thing that would cause their games to be erased.

Atari and Coleco left the videogame console business after the failures of the Jaguar and the Adam respectively, and both only exist as names now, not really stand-alone companies. Products are still sold bearing the brands, but only to capitalize on the nostalgic brands.

For a while, Sega ruled the video game roost with popular titles like the Sonic the Hedgehog games and Electronic Arts' popular John Madden football games. The Genesis dominated the market for the early '90s, but as the console market grew, it attracted attention from bigger players. As Sega replaced the Genesis with the ill-fated Dreamcast, Sony was beginning to take over the market with its PlayStation and Microsoft was readying the Xbox. With this heavy assault from Microsoft and Sony, coupled with the chilly reception the public gave the Dreamcast, Sega ultimately pulled out of the console market, choosing instead to focus on developing game titles.

Sony and Microsoft actually seemed to break the pattern of the video game console wars as they managed to release successful successor products. Sony has done so twice with the PlayStation 2 and again with the PlayStation 3. Microsoft actually improved its market position from the mild success of the original Xbox to the strong sustained success of the Xbox 360.

Of the early-generation video game companies, only Nintendo managed to recover from a misstep, while neither the Super Nintendo system or its follow-up, the GameCube, were market leaders, the company has long dominated the handheld market with its GameBoy product, which would have its own successful sequel, the DS. Though it no longer competes at the top of the console market, Nintendo also managed to become a major player in consoles with the Wii, which instead of offering the best graphics or the fanciest games, focused on a new kind of interactive controller.

The In-Car Phonograph: Take That, Eight-Tracks

Though vinyl records have largely disappeared as a format, at one point they were essentially the only method to listen to music. While the music snobs will talk about how "warm" the sound was on a record, the reality is that records were a clumsy format that, in addition to being awkward and large, were also prone to skips and jumps. Record players produced music by running a needle across the grooves on the record—which looked like a large plastic plate. Dance too hard or even take a strong step and that needle could "skip,"

DANIEL B. KLINE AND JASON TOMASZEWSKI

causing a break in the music or sometimes a squeaking noise that sounded like someone raking their nails down a chalkboard. Skips and jumps were facts of life with records, and it was not unheard of for a jump of the needle to literally change what song was playing.

That made record players ideally suited to well-fortified nonmoving places. The absolute worst possible place for a record player would, of course, be a moving vehicle. That probably explains why most—but not all—car companies wisely avoided installing record players in the vehicles. Chrysler, however, has never been deterred by pesky things like only installing add-ons that actually work in their vehicles, so in 1956, it offered a record player as an option on the DeSoto, Dodge, and Plymouth models.

To further add to the ridiculousness of this option, the in-dash record did not play the commonly available full-size records. Instead, it only played 45-speed records, which were essentially one song long on each side and a new format of seven-inch records that nobody actually produced any albums in. So not only was the integrity of the player and its ability to work correctly without skipping while moving highly doubtful, at best the players could play one song before the album needed to be flipped over.

The players were installed in the vehicles on a slide-out turntable beneath the dash, which was hidden behind a drop-down door that could be opened at the push of a button. It was possible to switch between the record player and the radio with a single switch, and both devices shared a volume knob as well as an equalizer.

As one might imagine, the systems did not work very well as records skipped whenever the vehicle hit a bumpy surface. Perhaps even worse, because the record players were made as part of an exclusive arrangement with Columbia Records, they could only play music from artists signed to that label. That made a ridiculous device pretty much useless as even if you simply used the player when parked, the extreme limitations of which artists you could listen to made it not worth the trouble of having one.

Laserdiscs: It's a DVD Mixed with a Record

Record-sized platters that could not actually hold most movies on one disc, laser discs were the most ridiculous of the half-baked formats that came before DVDs replaced VHS tapes and CDs replaced cassette tapes. The problem with any new format for delivering movies, music, or any other form of entertainment is that until enough people adopt it, prices will be absurdly high. The laser disc, however, made this problem part of its marketing pitch as laser discs were pushed as a high-end format for home theater snobs and others who appreciate the best quality.

The problem with marketing to the elite buyer is, of course, that only so many elite buyers exist. For a media format that quickly becomes a kiss of death as the limited market makes content providers wary of the format. Because only a tiny percentage of the movie-buying public had laser disc

players, only a limited amount of movies were released in the format, and those that were released cost three to five times more than their VHS cousins.

The laser disc actually began its life under the unfortunate name, "Discovision." Discovision, the format, which actually began in 1978, existed in near-total obscurity until Pioneer acquired it in the late 1980s. Though the format did become popular in Japan—where they seem to love ridiculous American castoffs—it never penetrated more than 2 percent of U.S. households. This was largely because laser disc players did not offer an appreciably better experience than the already inexpensive VHS that nearly every household already owned. Essentially, the makers of laser disc swere banking that people would pay hundreds of dollars for a format that did not really offer a better experience.

Laser discs did have better sound and higher picture quality than VHS tapes. Of course, to take advantage of those benefits, you needed a high-end television and a home theater audio system. Of course, since very few consumers had those, that meant that to get them to buy an already very expensive laser disc player, they also would have to spend thousands upgrading their televisions.

In addition to their costs, laser discs were literally the size of a record. This flew in the face of electronic trends where new products are almost always smaller than the ones they replace. Laser discs were the equivalent of Apple releasing a new iPod with slightly more storage and mildly better audio that was the size of a hardcover book. This size also meant that laser discs took up more shelf space in retail and rental stores, which also limited their availability. During the late '80s, "heyday" of laser discs, nearly every town had both chain and local video stores. These stores would have all the latest movies on VHS and one sorry shelf of laser discs, so even if you had a player and wanted to use it, rental choices were limited.

Perhaps the most damning characteristic of the laser disc was the fact that despite its large size, only sixty minutes of movie could be stored on each side. That meant that for average length movies, viewers would have to get up and flip the disc after an hour, and for long films, they would actually have to change the disc. That is, of course, if your laser discs were not subject (as many were) to "laser rot" whereby the glue holding the two sides of the disc together would come apart, rendering the already not-that-useful laser discs completely useless. Mercifully, the laser disc met a swift end as soon as the DVD was introduced.

Worst Electronic Gizmos Ever

- **Nintendo Virtual Boy**
  Looking like a giant bright red View-Master that completely cut off the wearer's vision, the Nintendo Virtual Boy was hyped as the first video game system to display "3-D graphics out of the box." Unfortunately, those 3-D graphics were rendered entirely in red LED pixels. The Virtual Boy gave users such bad headaches that Nintendo actually started recommending that people only play for fifteen minutes.

Only fourteen games were ever released in the United States, and no multiplayer games were ever released nor was the linking cable which made the Virtual Boy's EXT port completely useless. Nintendo pulled the much-hyped product in less than six months.

- DivX

 Sort of a competitor to movie rental stores, DivX was a DVD system where customers bought the disk for around $4.99. Once the disc was played, it was only good for forty-eight hours, making it essentially a rental that did not need to be returned. That all seemed great until consumers learned that playing DivX discs required a proprietary DVD player that cost hundreds of dollars. Essentially, you had to buy an expensive player to rent movies when you could already rent movies for less than the cost of a DivX disc pretty much anywhere.

- IBM PCjr

 A low-function computer with a keyboard that few could successfully type on, the PCjr was IBM's attempt to translate the success the company had experienced in the business world with the PC to the home market. The PCjr cost more than twice as much as the already popular Commodore 64 and was the same price as the similar Coleco Adam, which came with a printer, a tape drive, and software. In fact, the PC Jr. was so expensive that it was possible to buy a complete PC system from many of IBM's competitor for less than the cost of the very limited PC Jr.

- **N-Gage**

Not quite a cell phone, not quite a gaming system, the N-Gage was a Nokia product released in 2003 that was an attempt to lure customers away from Nintendo's Game Boy system by adding cell phone functionality. This, of course, failed, because the buttons required for a cell phone did not work well for a video game system, and trying to hold a video game system to your ear was awkward at best. It also didn't help that the N-Gage costs twice as much as Game Boy Advance and you also had to pay for phone service. In its first two weeks of availability, Nokia claimed four hundred thousand sold in the United States. In actuality, that number had been shipped to dealers, but only five thousand had actually been bought by customers.

- **Microsoft BOB**

  Introduced as a nontechnical method to navigate the already pretty nontechnical Microsoft Windows environment, BOB was supposedly a way for Microsoft to make its products more user-friendly. Released in 1995, the software put users in a virtual house where they could use various icons to launch software like word processors and financial planners. This simplistic interface not only insulted the people it was aimed at by treating them like children but turned them off from computers in general by making them seem cartoonish and not all that useful. Microsoft would later repeat this mistake by adding the paper clip cartoon to Word whose only success was in teaching a revolted audience how to quickly turn him off.

The Female Urinal: Finally, Women Can Pee Standing Up

The best worst products solve a problem that nobody knew existed. The female urinal does exactly that as it's a plastic coated funnel contraption that allows women to pee standing up. This valuable skill, formerly reserved only for those who actually possess a penis, might come in handy for women every now and then, but it seems unlikely that most women (or any) would carry around what is essentially a plastic funnel that sort of molds over the female genitalia just in case an appropriate situation should arise.

A shocking number of different versions of the female urinal have been marketed, but all provide essentially the same function—they allow women to pee standing up. One such product, the now-defunct La Femme, touted this as beneficial to women stuck waiting in line at bars while men—due to their ability to pee standing up—quickly cycled in and out of the bathroom.

This idea, of course, assumed that men would not mind a woman walking up next to him in a crowded bar bathroom, dropping her pants (or lifting her skirt), placing a plastic device over her ladyparts and using said urinal. Even in a single gender situation urinals can be uncomfortable places. In venues like bars or stadiums where the bathrooms are crowded, most men have to be careful to keep their eyes forward in order to avoid an uncomfortable view of their neighbor. Most men would likely not want a woman sharing this experience with them and those that would, well, I'm guessing women would not want to be semi-unclothed next to them.

Of course, the devices not only allow women to use urinals, they also allow them to make use of alternate facilities—such as walls or parking lots as men have often done. Women, though, are generally a little more discreet than men and other than in dire emergencies (when you are unlikely to be carrying your helpful pee device anyway) very little demand exists for women to have the ability to pee while standing up.

In addition, most of these devices were relatively poorly made—basically cheap sleeves of plastic. Using them required keeping them in place. A slight deviation in the use of the product and the woman who had ostensibly been using the device to not have urine all over herself would have urine spraying about.

Though a number of companies have tried to create these devices and numerous versions have been released commercially, none have caught on or even really been part of the public consciousness. So, for now, urinals remain male only with women being forced to wait in lines, while peeing in a communal trough stays strictly the provence of the rougher gender.

THE "ARTS"

Jar Jar Binks: "Mesa" the Worst Character Ever

Following in the sad tradition of the Ewoks, Jar Jar Binks represented another attempt by George Lucas to bring young kids into the Star Wars universe. An attempt at comic relief in the three Star Wars prequels, Binks became almost universally reviled by fans of the movies. Despite his goofy appearance and bumbling heroism, Jar Jar never became the Star Wars version of Elmo that Lucas and his marketing people likely envisioned.

With giant floppy ears and bulging eyestalks, Binks looked preposterous in a world where Chewbacca and Jabba the Hut fit in fine. There was nothing subtle about Jar Jar. Even a little kid could look at him onscreen and see him as a toy walking amongst movie characters. Lucas might as well have introduced Strawberry Shortcake or Teddy Ruxpin as a companion for Anakin Skywalker, and the intent would not have been any less obvious.

Speaking in a vaguely offensive mix of gibberish and a Caribbean dialect, Binks was not only disliked, but many fans considered him a racist caricature. Many viewed him as a bad black stereotype, sort of the intergalactic version of Ted Danson in blackface or other well-intentioned, but woefully inappropriate ideas. Lines like "Mesa day startin' pretty okee-day with a brisky morning munchen, then boom! Gettin' berry scared and grabbin' dat Jedi and pow! Mesa here! Mesa gettin' berry, berry scared!" delivered in Binks's faux-island accent did not help this portrayal.

Binks may be the only failed character in Star Wars history as even the kids he was supposed to entertain largely rejected him. Though many adults dismissed the Ewoks as giant teddy bears in *Return of the Jedi*, kids latched onto the characters, which not only broadened the appeal of the film, it sold a lot of merchandise. The difference, perhaps, is that while the Ewoks looked like teddy bears, their actions were intentional. They might have been cute and fuzzy, but their heroism on the battlefield was undeniable. Binks, on the other hand, was portrayed as a bumbling idiot—like the pretty girl in an action movie who only helps when she trips and accidentally fires the gun that she otherwise does not know how to use.

Binks became even more ridiculous when, as the trilogy progressed, he moved from exiled incompetent—an example of the worst of his species—to Galactic Senator. Since there was no way to keep him in the plot as a bumbling fool on the battlefield, Jar Jar's accidental heroism apparently made him a hero to his people. This newfound renown led them to elect him as their representative to the Star Wars equivalent of Congress. This made no sense as his own people knew him to be an idiot—a well-intentioned idiot certainly, but an idiot nonetheless.

Despite the almost instant revulsion most *Star Wars* fans felt for the character, Lucas featured him in all three prequels and continues to use Jar Jar as a supporting character in *The Clone Wars* television show. And, of course, every manner of Jar Jar Binks toy exists, from dolls and action figures to an umbrella and an alarm clock that's perfect for anyone who wants to be woken by a vaguely racist puppet.

Celebrity Albums: Being Famous Does Not Make You a Good Singer

They say that every singer wants to be an actor and every actor wants to be a singer. "Want" and "should," however, are two very different words, and though a lot of actors have released albums, very few were a good idea. Of course, just because an actor has no particular musical talent does not mean that he or she cannot release an album. If you're famous enough, you not only get to put out a CD, you might even have a hit single.

Perhaps the most egregious offender in this genre of nonsingers with enough hubris to insist on releasing not one but multiple albums would be comedian Eddie Murphy. At the height of his popularity, coming off the success of *Beverly Hills Cop*, Murphy released the album *How Can It Be,* featuring the ridiculous single "Party All the Time." Despite Murphy's inability to carry a tune, this song hit number 2 on the Billboard Top 100. Not content to simply have one novelty hit, Murphy struck again in 1989 with the mercifully forgotten *So Happy,* which included the single "Put Your Mouth on Me," a song that went to number two on the R & B charts.

Murphy, however, saved his best for last as in 1993, he released his final (we hope) album *Love's Alright,* featuring a duet with Michael Jackson "Whatzupwitu." Despite featuring the "King of Pop," and receiving heavy video rotation on MTV, this single and album went nowhere, forcing Murphy into making countless movies where he dons a fatsuit. It's hard to quantify which was a worse choice, recording "Whatzupwitu" or making *Norbit*, but both leave you feeling a little sick to your stomach.

Murphy was not alone amongst big stars releasing albums because nobody in their entourage had the guts to tell them they could not sing. Among those committing this sin was Bruce

Willis, who released three records, but only got attention for 1987's *Return of Bruno*, which included the minor hit "Respect Yourself." Also in the one-hit album category, despite not being able to sing, was Willis's fellow 1980s television star Don Johnson, who charted with the single "Heartbeat" from the 1986 album of the same name. Johnson returned in 1988 with the song "Till I Loved You," a duet with Barbra Streisand that proved that gay people won't actually buy anything Ms. Streisand releases.

Not being as big a star as Murphy or Willis did not stop Joe Pesci from mortgaging his fame for a record deal as in 1998. In 1998, he released *Vincent LaGuardia Gambini Sings Just for You*, which spawned the single "Wise Guy." Almost impossibly bad, "Wise Guy," played off the gangster theme of many of Pesci's movies. The song sampled Blondie's "Rapture" and was one of two songs of note on the album, the other being Pesci's tribute to his own signature character, "Yo Cousin Vinny."

You do not, of course, need to be a big star to release a CD, though it does appear to help album sales. Reality "star" Heidi Montag only managed to sell 658 copies of her album *Superficial* in its first week of release. That may actually be more than Kevin Federline sold of his *Playing with Fire,* an album that perhaps nobody actually purchased.

Adding a Cute Kid: The Last Gasp of a Dying Sitcom

After all the stunt-casting cameos (look everyone it's Cher and Gilligan from *Gilligan's Island)* and all the "very special" episdoes ("I know the dog has cancer, but as a family, we can help him pull through) sometimes the only remaining trick a sitcom with declining appeal can pull is the addition of a new, cute kid. Normally this happens on family shows which were built around the concept of the kids in the family being endearingly cute. Unfortunately, Hollywood is not legally allowed to stunt kids growth or give them drugs to keep

them the same age (this law is unofficially known as "Emanuel Lewis' Law" so invariably the kids on sitcoms get older.

Sometimes this works out as Alyssa Milano went from cute kid to super-hot in the blink of an eye and even the Olsen twins went from super-cute babies to cute teens, but usually it goes a lot more like it did for other kids on *Who's the Boss* and *Full House*. As cute kids get older, nearly everyone, even those on hit TV shows tend to go through an awkward period. For some, this is a temporary thing, but for others (Leif Garrett comes to mind) it turns out that those good-looking early years were just a tease. That can be difficult for regular people, but when your awkward years plays out on national television, ratings tend to fall. People love to tune in to see what the cute kid with the lisp might say, they are less interested in watching the pimply kid with braces who still has a lisp.

Generally, a hit sitcom lasts between five and eight years. In most cases (*Seinfeld* and *Friends* being the notable exceptions) show tend to peak somewhere in the middle of their runs. After that, it becomes a battle to stay on the air as the cost to run a show goes up each year and if ratings fall, eventually the studio decides to pul the plug.

One of the most desperate tricks in the sitcom world is adding a new younger kid to the cast as a way to recapture that original magic. Invariably this fails as fans of the show see through the transparent ploy and reject the new character. This ploy also fails because network bosses are greedy. Instead of merely hiring a cute kid or a kid who does something cute (like the aforementioned lisp) they get an impossibly cute kid full of ticks and "cute" mannerisms.

Perhaps the worst of these was when Raven Symone joined the cast of *The Cosby Show* as Cliff Huxtable's grandaughter Olivia. Symone was needed because Keisha Knight Pulliam, who had previously been the cute kid "Rudy," she had gotten older and was no longer nearly as cute or as endearing. And, since everyone wanted to see "The 'Cos" interact with an adorable little kid, Symone was brought in.

And, boy was she cute, with her baby voice and her impossibly endearing mannerisms, but Symone was too much of a good thing as she was so sickly sweet that you could now get diabetes watching the show. Whereas *The Cosby Show* had been a realistic portrait of an upper-middle class African American family, it now became Bill Cosby and the cute kid. This was, of course, not the only reason for the decline of the show (the plots got more and more ridiculous as the years went on) but it did not help.

In addition to the actual kids being introduced to these shows being a bad idea, often the story used to bring them on board was especially preposterous. The best of these might be the often forgotten role future box office king and heartthrob Leonardo DiCaprio played on one-time hit sitcom *Growing Pains*. With Kirk Cameron rejecting his teen idol status in favor of becoming a religious nut and Tracey Gold becoming an anorexic, DiCaprio was brought on board during the show's final season as "Luke Brower," a homeless boy adopted by the Seavers. Not only was this a craven attempt to shoehorn a new cute kid into the show, it was also seen as impossibly lame because while the audience new Mr. and Mrs. Seaver were good parents, it was impossible to believe that anyone would randomly adopt a homeless kid and if they did, would he really look like Leonardo DiCaprio? How many homeless kids have hundred dollar hair-cuts and perfect teeth?

The most egregious offense of jamming a kid into a failing show happened on *The Brady Bunch,* which was sort of a mix between a sitcom and a drama. That show had been built around the idea of having six adorable kids of varying ages and, well, as they aged, let's just say that at least Maureen McCormick (Marsha) still looked good. The youngest kids, however, "Bobby" and "Cindy," did not fair nearly as well, hence the addition of "cousin Oliver."

Played by 9-year-old Robbie Rist, cousin Oliver came to live with the Bradys for what would turn out to be their last six episodes. With his John Denver bowl cut and glasses, Rist was supposed to be dorkishly cute, but instead, he was just oddly uncomfortable. The addition of cousin Oliver basically drew a giant arrow to the older kids and pointed out exactly how not cute Susan Olsen (Cindy) had become. Oliver was a spectacular failure and the show was quickly cancelled, though it would be brought back in a number of forms over the years (none of which acknowledged the existence of cousin Oliver, who know lives with Richie Cunningham's older brother Chuck in a special house for TV characters whose existence has been completely denied).

CBS Radio Lets Howard Stern Go to Satellite: How to End Your Company in One Contract

O
ver twenty-plus years, Howard Stern built a radio empire. Not only was he at the top of the ratings heap in New York, where his show originated, he had the number one morning radio program in major markets around the country. Though he constantly ran afoul of the FCC, he produced hundreds of millions of dollars for his employer CBS Radio.

More than just a successful morning radio program, *The Howard Stern Show* provided a financial base for the stations it aired on. Not just a cash cow in the morning, Stern's ratings success propped up the rest of the day for the mostly rock-music formatted stations that carried his show.

During most of Stern's terrestrial radio run, he had few opportunities to leave that would dramatically change his situation. Sure, he could switch companies or stations, but there were only so many major players in radio, and while his bosses at CBS Radio were often less-than-supportive, it seemed unlikely that any other company would treat him much better.

Because of the controversy and FCC scrutiny that went along with employing Stern, his career options were limited despite his massive success. This, of course, led his employer to treat him shabbily. Though he was certainly well paid, Stern never received anywhere near fair value for the money he brought into the company. This was partly because his bosses considered him a headache and partially because radio executives view talent as interchangeable no matter how well they do in the ratings. If Stern were to leave CBS, the station bosses could just find another person to put in the chair.

Perhaps it was that thinking that stopped CBS Radio from truly making an effort to keep Stern. Though he was offered a new contract, Stern never received assurances that his employer would back him in any fights with the FCC. Instead of putting themselves squarely in their star employee's corner, bowling him over financially and generally showing Stern the appreciation he deserved, CBS Radio basically just let him go.

In doing so, they essentially signed their own death warrant.

When Stern left, he made the seemingly curious decision to pick the much smaller Sirius satellite radio company over its much larger rival XM. CBS assumed this was another mistake on Stern's part—he would essentially be going to a platform with no listeners that cost money. They would still be free, and listeners would certainly accept whoever they put in Stern's chair instead of paying $12 a month to follow Stern.

When he left, it was estimated that Stern was responsible for 10 percent of CBS Radio's total revenue. At his flagship station, WXRK, he brought in 75 percent of the $75 million a year the station billed. Those numbers proved to be an understatement as his replacements dragged the company quickly to the bottom.

First, David Lee Roth and Adam Carolla were brought in to host in various parts of the country. As that failed, Opie & Anthony—sort of younger Stern knockoffs—were given the slot. When they failed, the wheels quickly came off the bus, and most of Stern's former stations were gutted. WXRK even dropped rock and became a Top 40 station while Boston's long-running rock station WBCN simply went out of business.

As this was happening and nearly every decision maker at CBS Radio was replaced, Stern was busy turning Sirius from a tiny gnat buzzing around traditional radio to a behemoth. The company, which had around six hundred thousand subscribers when Stern joined, swelled quickly into multiple millions then ten million and ultimately, twenty million when they merged with XM.

So in letting Stern go, not only did CBS Radio lose their signature personality, causing nearly every station that carried his show to plummet in the ratings. They also allowed the "king of all media" to take a rival that likely would have run out of money and gone away into a viable competitor. Over five years later, CBS and terrestrial radio in general have not recovered and short of Stern returning, it seems unlikely they ever will.

Jay Leno Moves to 10:00 PM: Don't Worry, Conan, Everyone at NBC Loves Your Show

When NBC made the deal in 2004 that would have Jay Leno hand the reigns of *The Tonight Show* to Conan O'Brien, one could only assume that network brass never expected to be around in five years to sort out the mess they had created. In announcing that Leno was being pushed out, albeit very slowly, they could not possibly have imagined that five years later, he would still have the number one show at 11:35PM, and that he would not actually want to leave.

At the time, the solution seemed brilliant. The network would keep Leno on *The Tonight Show* for five more years, and Conan O'Brien would not leave for ABC or Fox. Jeff Zucker, then CEO of NBC, likely assumed that O'Brien's appeal would continue to grow after he got named heir apparent, and Leno's would start to fade as he got older. Unfortunately for him, the opposite happened as O'Brien started occasionally losing to Craig

Ferguson in the ratings and Leno strengthened his lead over David Letterman.

Zucker, however, had painted himself into a corner, as if NBC did not give O'Brien *The Tonight Show* at the designated time the network owed him a massive payment in the $35–40 million range. In addition to the huge payday, O'Brien would also be able to take his talents to Fox or ABC—both of which seemed eager to establish a late-night franchise.

If O'Brien got the show as planned, though, Leno—the ratings leader—would be free to go to ABC or Fox. Under this doomsday scenario, not only would NBC lose Leno, he would become a competitor and likely take his audience with him. Furthermore, Leno had spent the five years since what he considered his firing, getting more and more angry at the situation. He wanted to continue hosting *The Tonight Show* and though he had loyalty, if not to NBC at least to his work routine, the comedian did not understand why he was being pushed aside while he still led the ratings race.

As the five years ended, Zucker offered Leno a number of scenarios to keep him at the network. These included ideas like hosting specials or having a weekly show. The idea of Leno hosting a daily show on one of NBC's cable networks was floated as well, but none of them appealed to Leno. With time running out and the concept of Jay moving to another network imminent, Zucker offered him a show five nights a week at 10:00PM

In theory, since Leno at 10:00PM would be cheaper to produce than the hour-long dramas like *Law & Order* or *ER* that traditionally filled that time slot, it would not have to do as well in the ratings. Plus, Leno and Zucker said, since the competition only produced new shows twenty-two weeks a year or so, Leno's lack of vacations would result in him doing well while other shows were in repeats. If Leno's late-night audience followed him, they suggested, they would have a successful show, albeit not a traditional hit.

This all makes sense if you only consider the 10:00PM time period. If you project out what lower ratings will mean to the local affiliates who make a lot of money on their 11:00PM newscasts, then, well, you have a disaster. While moving Leno to 10:00PM kept him from going elsewhere, it immediately changed NBC

from the network that brought some of the best dramas in history to the guys who gave up on the ten o'clock hour. It also put affiliates on edge, making it not unsurprising when they quickly revolted once the ratings started coming in.

Leno's sleepy brand of inoffensive humor seemed especially bland at 10:00 PM, and his audience did not follow him. This led to poor lead-ins for both the local affiliates and O'Brien's *Tonight Show*. Conan officially had *The Tonight Show*, but he was still hosting the second show of the night on NBC crippled by poor ratings and spotty network support.

After a few months, changes clearly had to be made, and Zucker, ever the peacemaker, attempted to move Leno to a half hour show at eleven thirty with Conan's *Tonight Show* pushed back to midnight. O'Brien considered this for about thirty seconds before realizing he was being asked to move into another impossible position, so he resigned taking $35 million from NBC and becoming a folk hero to his audience.

A damaged act due to the ratings failure of his *Tonight Show* stint (albeit much of the blame can be laid on his poor lead-in), essentially getting, fired reinvigorated O'Brien. Not only did ratings explode for his last few weeks on *The Tonight Show*, but the host became a symbol to his core audience. They rallied behind him with "I'm with Coco" pins and supported his sold-out live tour. They also supported his new show—surprisingly on TBS, not ABC or Fox—where he drew sizable ratings, fracturing the late-night audience, and hastening Leno's decline.

Now back on *The Tonight Show*, Leno no longer has a stranglehold on the ratings, he loses to Letterman regularly, and Conan trounces him with the younger demographics. Zucker, of course, lost his job, though the fact that he survived as long as he did was pretty impressive in the first place.

Late-Night Disasters

- *The Magic Hour*. There was no particular reason to believe that Magic Johnson would be an engaging talk show host. Though he was a likeable enough personality, Johnson was not a particularly good basketball analyst, so it was met with universal surprise when it was announced that Johnson would be hosting a talk show. That surprise quickly turned into disgust as Johnson proved ill at ease, not really interested in his guests, and generally uncomfortable. The short-lived show had exactly one highlight—an appearance by Howard Stern where he took over the interview and ridiculed the host.

- *The Chevy Chase Show.* At least Chevy Chase had been on TV before Fox named him their latest attempt at breaking into the lucrative world of late-night talk shows. The network had already tried and failed with Joan Rivers, who at least had a history of doing well filling in for Johnny Carson, and had actually offered the show to Dolly Parton before giving it to Chase. That proved a disaster as the show was widely panned by critics and was cancelled after four weeks. That cancellation was  hastened by Fox, having promised its affiliates five to six million viewers—more than Carson or David Letterman was doing at the time.

- *The Keenen Ivory Wayans Show.* In its eleven episode run, it was impossible to know if Keenen Ivory Wayans was a good talk show host or not because he encouraged his audience to hoot and holler through the entire program. Wayans did find time to talk—immediately after he asked a guest a question—proving that having the audience drown him out was a good idea.

- *ALF's Hit Talk Show.* Only Kermit the Frog as a substitute for Larry King has ever made the difficult, puppet-to-talk-show-host crossover. ALF proved a likeable host, mocking sidekick Ed McMahon (yes, that Ed McMahon) for how low his career had sunk Sadly, the audience could only bear seeing a puppet interview D-list celebrities while making cat-eating jokes for so long, and the show was cancelled after seven episodes.

Battlefield Earth: Religious Cult Spawns Sci-Fi Bomb

For at least two stretches in his career, John Travolta has been one of the biggest stars on the planet. He had an early run during the *Saturday Night Fever* days and then a second run at the top of the A-list after *Pulp Fiction* rescued him from making more talking-baby movies. When a star produces hits so consistently, he generally gets a lot of power, and this gives him the ability to make movies that nobody thinks are good ideas. Occasionally, this works out (Mel Gibson's *Passion of the Christ*) but usually it does not (Mel Gibson's *Apocolypto*).

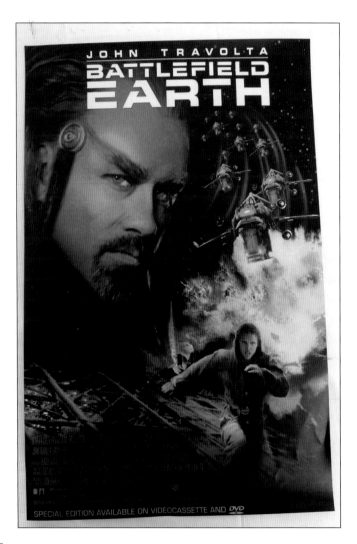

Generally, however, it is taken as a really bad sign when a star of Travolta's standing can't get any traditional Hollywood outlet to finance his pet project.

In many cases, studios will make a movie they don't want to make with a star in the hopes (or the contractual promise) that the star will return the favor. Still, nobody wanted to work with Travolta enough to green-light *Battlefield Earth* even if he did agree to appear in other movies. Not willing to be defeated by the collected wisdom of everyone else in the movie business, Travolta instead pulled another move that big stars can use to make vanity projects—he raised the money from clueless rich people who wanted some way into the movie business. And though it's probably little comfort to those investors who ultimately went bankrupt, Travolta believed in the project so much that he invested millions of his own dollars in the movie.

Studios, and all of Hollywood, did not want to make *Battlefield Earth* because it was the lightly regarded work of former science-fiction writer L. Ron Hubbard. Never really highly thought of as a writer, Hubbard would later go on to essentially declare himself the Messiah and create the religion of Scientology. Creating a religion is, of course, a fairly impressive feat, but that does not automatically make your earlier work better. Even this did not deter Travolta—a devout Scientologist—from adapting the novel for the big screen.

Battlefield Earth, of course, had strong Scientology undertones. In fact, calling them undertones would actually be an insult to subtlety as they were right there on the surface. Fortunately, Scientologists are so secretive as to what they actually believe that even clumsy, over-the-top messaging jammed into a sci-fi movie gets lost on the general public.

The movie was about an Earth that has been under the rule of the alien Psychlos for one thousand years. (Psychlos were giant aliens with dreadlocks—they sort of looked like Predator if a kid had made his Predator costume with a very limited budget). The story involved a rebellion by the human population, which had been enslaved by the Psychlos to mine gold. There were small pockets of free humans who had basically reverted into primitive behaviors, living in remote areas the Psychlos could not be bothered to take over.

It is, of course, one of those free humans, Jonnie (played by former actor Barry Pepper), who attempts to free humanity where he comes into contact with the evil Terl (Travolta) a sort of outcast Psychlo who has been forced by his bosses to supervise the entire Earth-enslaving operation. Even more villainous than his pretty evil fellow Psychlos, Terl devises a way to end his banishment by forcing the

humans to mine gold in radioactive areas. Conveniently, Psychlos can't go anywhere near these areas because despite their monstrous builds, they have delicate constitutions that succumb easily to radiation.

In this long and convoluted story, Terl selects Jonnie as the foreman for this project seemingly as punishment but blatantly obviously as a way for Jonnie to have a little space to put a rebellion together. Like a Batman villain insisting upon setting up the Caped Crusader to be turned into taffy or maybe be eaten by sharks—then leaving, assuming his plan will work—Terl basically gives Jonnie all the tools needed to eventually overthrow the Psychlos. This included educating him using one of those magic sci-fi plot device rapid education montages. In this montage, he not only teaches Jonnie the Psychlos language but points out that they can't go near the radiation because it causes an explosive reaction with the gas they breathe while on Earth.

Conveniently, the mine site—which Terl cannot visit—sits atop an abandoned underground U.S. Military base with working aircraft, weapons, fuel, and nuclear weapons. Mind you, these weapons must be hundreds of years old, yet they work perfectly, including the flight simulators, which Jonnie and his rebel crew use to teach themselves how to fly high-tech jets in a manner of days. Of course, the good guys find a way to defeat the bad guys, even managing to teleport a nuclear bomb back to the Psychlo home planet, killing everyone there (let's assume their entire population was evil and the Earth occupation wasn't the product of some bad-egg Psychlos).

The movie cost over $75 million to make and another $25 million to market while making just under $30 million worldwide.

Vanity Projects Gone Wrong

- *Glitter*
Take an established star in music and put him/her in either a literal or a thinly-veiled version of his/her own life, and the public would surely lap it up. Sadly, though, for every Eminem in *8 Mile,* there were countless Vanilla Ices in *Cool as Ice.* Still, this did not stop Twentieth Century Fox from casting Mariah Carey in *Glitter*, a poorly scripted film that was essentially Carey's life story. Hopes were high for the movie, but nobody bothered to check, before making it, whether Carey could act or whether she was emotionally stable enough to star in a movie.

  It turned out she wasn't, as the film's release over the lucrative Labor Day weekend after Carey had to be hospitalized during the promotional run-up to the film for "extreme exhaustion." This followed a bizarre appearance on MTV's then hugely influential *Total Request Live* where she spoke incoherently and attempted a strip tease for the show's young teen audience.

Glitter was widely panned by critics, and despite Carey's fame and the hype surrounding the movie, it made only just over $2 million in its opening weekend. Ultimately, the movie grossed about $5 million worldwide on a budget (not counting marketing expenses) of $25 million.

- *The Postman* and *Waterworld*

  Kevin Costner earned himself an enormous amount of Hollywood benefit of the doubt when he went against pretty much the entire industry and turned *Dancing with Wolves* into a critically acclaimed megahit. Sadly, however, those instincts proved to be the exception rather than the rule as Costner's next two attempts to go against conventional wisdom resulted in two of the biggest financial failures in box office history.

  The first, *Waterworld,* was more or less *Mad Max* set in the ocean. Costner's character was a weird hybrid who had both gills and lungs as well as an unflattering ponytail that, it was rumored, had to be painted in during postproduction so Costner's alleged bald spots would not show through. *The Postman* was also set in a postapocalyptic world, and the plot was even less entertaining as Costner played a drifter who finds an old United States Postal Service uniform, which he uses to convince people that the United States was back in business and help was coming against their warlord overlords.

The Postman had an $80 million budget and made just over $17 million worldwide. *Waterworld* made more money (around $88 million), but its then incredible $175 million production budget made it an even larger money loser.

- *Gigli*

In 2003, Jennifer Lopez and Ben Affleck were huge movie stars who happened to be dating. They were dubbed "Bennifer" by the press, and their huge celebrity created demand for their first starring roles together, and made the resulting movie *Gigli* a highly anticipated release. Unfortunately, at some point during the making of the movie, the public grew tired of the couple. Still, they were both very famous and had headlined successful movies, so if the film was good, the backlash could be averted. Sadly, the film was not good; in fact, it was epically bad and the public responded in kind. *Gigli* not only made just barely $6 million on a production budget of $54 million, it also ruined the box office chances for the movie *Jersey Girl*. That film, an infinitely better one than *Gigli*, made by indie director and Affleck friend, Kevin Smith, only featured Lopez in a tiny scene with Affleck, but that was enough, and *Jersey Girl* struggled to make $25 million on its $35 million budget.

Cop Rock: Police and Musical Numbers Don't Mix

While a lot of bad ideas have made it onto American airwaves (*My Mother the Car,* about a deceased mom reincarnated as a car, and *Cavemen*, starring the Geico cavemen, come to mind) none were as amazingly awful—in both idea and execution—as *Cop Rock*. At first, the series seemed to be a novel idea with an impressive pedigree. The series was developed by Stephen Bochco, the mind behind *Hill Street Blues, L.A. Law,* and *NYPD Blue*. Basically, this was a guy who knew how to run a cop show, and how bad could anything that he conceived and developed be?

The answer was, of course, perhaps the worst show of all time. Though the title suggests a show about police who play in a band on the side or maybe officers who specialize in music-related crimes, the reality was, in fact, much worse. *Cop Rock* was part police procedural, part bombastic Broadway musical. These two genres were not an easy match—think salad and ice cream—and the resulting program was an uncomfortable mess where any time the audience became invested in the story, that momentum would be crushed by a musical number.

Imagine watching an hour of *Law & Order,* becoming invested in the courtroom drama, and as the tension rises as to what the jury will say, they deliver their verdict in song. "He's Guilty" was an actual song on the show, which also included an opening musical sequence by Randy Newman. Other songs included Hispanic defendants launching into song, suggesting that their arrests were due to racism, and some episodes even feature Sheryl Crow as a background singer.

Perhaps the most amazing thing about *Cop Rock* was that ABC actually aired eleven episodes of the show, which routinely tops lists of the worst TV programs of all time. Perhaps because of its profound awfulness, *Cop Rock* has had a bit of a *Rocky Horror Picture Show*–style afterlife. Instead of merely disappearing, the series has had runs on a number of cable outlets on VH1, A&E, and Trio.

Viva Laughlin

Before the surprising success of *Glee* briefly gave the TV networks the idea that people wanted to see shows that mixed musical numbers with reality, CBS tried the genre, failing in *Cop Rock*-esque fashion. *Glee*, which came a few years later, works because the premise naturally leads to characters performing songs, but those premises are hard to come by, and mixing music and drama most certainly did not work for CBS's *Viva Laughlin.*

Based on a popular British series, *Viva Laughlin* was a short-lived CBS series, which was cancelled after a mere two episodes in 2007 despite having Hollywood heavy-hitter Hugh "Wolverine" Jackman as one of its executive producers. Perhaps the show failed because murder mysteries do not naturally lend themselves to song. Police detectives investigating gruesome murders rarely break out into song, and there was no natural way to shoehorn giant production numbers into the plotline.

The mystery centered on businessman Ripley Holden and his attempts to open a casino. This effort has required every dime he has, and when, at the last minute his financing falls through, he must approach his hated rival, the lazily named Nicky

Fontanna for help. Fontanna, of course, wants to own the casino by himself, and Holden turns down the deal, at which point, Fontanna gets murdered, and lots of singing ensued.

Though it was cancelled quickly, *Viva Laughlin* was not criticized for its musical numbers the way *Cop Rock* had been. Instead, critics blasted the horrible scripts, bad acting, and generally awful dialogue. Though Jackman has gone on to prove his musical credibility hosting the Tonys and later the Oscars, *Viva Laughlin* has yet to be revived even in an ironic, "so bad it's good" fashion.

Godfather Part III: Too Much of a Good Thing

Sequels almost never live up to the original film. In fact, most sequels are just a pretty obvious way for everyone involved to cash in on the notoriety of the original movie. That makes it very impressive that the success of the original *The Godfather* was followed by *The Godfather Part II*. Both films were not only commercially successful, but both won best picture Oscars and are considered all-time classics.

Following two best picture winners made it nearly impossible for *The Godfather Part III* to meet expectations. It's sort of

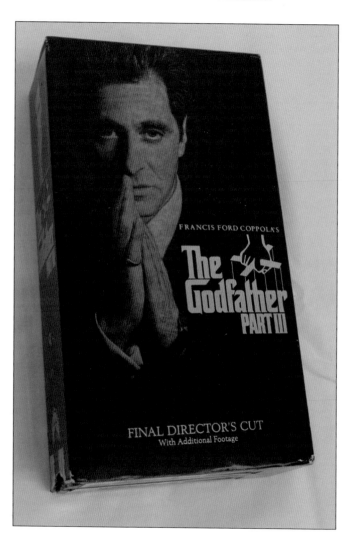

like if you just dated two supermodels, it would be hard to go back to dating that pretty girl at work. She might have been perfectly gorgeous had you seen her before you met the supermodels, but now, well, you know what filet mignon tastes like, so it's hard to go back to burgers.

The first two *Godfather* films both draw from the novel *The Godfather* by Mario Puzo. The third, though it maintains the story lines of the novel, does not actually follow a story in the book. The third film also requires that you watch the first two if you want the movie to make any sense. That, of course, happens with sequels, but in most cases even the most story-driven epics (think *Empire Strikes Back* or *Indiana Jones and the Temple of Doom*) still make sense to a new audience once they get the characters straight. With *The Godfather Part III*, the film was simply too dense to watch on its own if you had not seen the first two.

In the case of many enormously successful trilogies, this would not be a problem as the large audiences that loved the first two would see the third one. That might produce a slightly declining audience, but the crowds would still be large. Unfortunately, that system presupposes that the films all get released within a few years of each other. In the case of *The Godfather* films, the first was released in 1972, the second in 1974, and the third in 1990.

Today, that might not be a problem because in the endless cable universe, it seems there are periods where *The Godfather* movies are always playing. In 1990, however, that was not the case as there were many less cable outlets, many fewer people with cable and, though the movies were available on video, only a small percentage of the potential audience was reaching back sixteen and eighteen years respectively to watch the first two movies.

In addition to having story problems and a huge gap since the first two movies had been popular, *The Godfather Part III* had another huge problem—Sofia Coppola. The daughter of the *Godfather* series director, Francis Ford Coppola, Sofia was not considered an actress by the general public. Her casting in a film where she would play a pivotal role alongside multiple Oscar winners was considered ludicrous and was widely panned before a single frame of her appeared on-screen. A complete unknown might have been questioned, but the director casting his own daughter was met with the reaction that Woody Allen would get if he cast himself in the lead in a remake of *Gladiator*.

Sofia Copolla, who would later go on to become a successful director herself with *Lost in Translation,* was universally panned in the movie and her casting was seen as absurd nepotism. And while the first two movies won Best Picture Oscars, *The Godfather Part III* won two Golden Raspberry Awards, both for Sofia Coppola for Worst Supporting Actress and Worst New Star.

Other Dubious Sequels

- *Superman IV*: The Quest for Peace

  Even though *Superman III* featured Richard Pryor, a killer computer, and tobacco-laced synthetic kryptonite not to mention a plot that pitted an evil Superman against a good Clark Kent in a no-holds-barred junkyard battle, that was not the worst *Superman* sequel. That honor instead goes to *Superman IV: The Quest for Peace*, a sort of Cold War analogy that had Superman (powered by the sun) battling the evil Nuclear Man (powered by villainous capitalists and their dangerous nuclear energy). Nuclear Man also had a ridiculous black-and-gold leotard that was supposed to look menacing, but mostly looked like he stole it from a lower-end Mexican wrestler. This was also the *Superman* where they cheaped out, so to say the special effects are amateur would be an insult to amateurs who would at least cover up the wires that made the hero fly.

- *Star Wars: The Phantom Menace*

  The first three *Star Wars* movies have inspired one of the most devoted fan-bases in the history of moviedom. Fans were literally begging George Lucas to make more of them, and he responded by delivering a prequel trilogy. Though two of the movies were legitimately bad (only *Revenge of the Sith* is defensible), the worst of the three was the ponderous *Phantom Menace*. Not only did the movie feature a

LOGRAY™ AND CHIEF CHIRPA™

young Anakin Skywalker, well before his journey to becoming Darth Vader, it also featured endless debate scenes that bored everyone. Perhaps most egregious, the movie featured Jar Jar Binks, a CGI alien character who spoke in Ebonics and made the Ewoks seem macho.

- *Blues Brothers 2000*

This might have worked, except John Belushi was dead and even Jim Belushi had the sense to turn this piece of dreck down. Jim Belushi—the man who made *K-9*—turned this down, yet it still got made. The plot, if you can call it that, was basically just an excuse for two old guys Dan Aykroyd and John

Goodman to wear suits and pretend they were still cool. They weren't, and this was truly embarrassing.

- *Caddyshack II*

If there's a truly awful sequel, there's a decent chance it stars Dan Aykroyd. He's in this too, but you know who isn't? Bill Murray. Instead, we get Jackie Mason, which is like trading in a Jaguar for a used Huffy.

- *Rocky V*

Rocky IV was ridiculous (that's the one where he essentially defeated communism), but at least it followed the basic story arc of "Rocky trains hard and wins an impossible-to-win fight." This sequel, however, has Rocky broken and brain-damaged, working as a trainer to the charisma-free Tommy Morrison as villain Tommy Gunn. Mr. T had chains with more personality than this guy. Sadly, the movie does not culminate in a big boxing match. Instead, Balboa and Gunn have a street fight that weirdly had rounds.

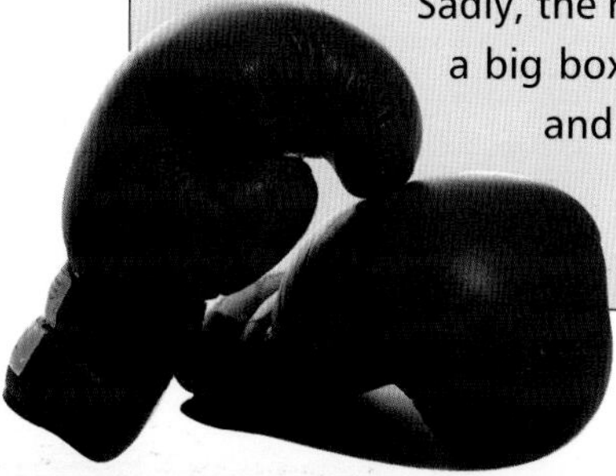

Theodore Rex: Whoopi Goldberg and a Dinosaur Puppet Make $35 Million Disappear

While it's easy to imagine a Hollywood agent pitching "it's *Jurassic Park* meets *Lethal Weapon*," it's hard to picture a studio not only buying the script but committing $35 million to a movie about a human cop paired with an animatronic dinosaur. It's even harder to imagine that the studio (in this case New Line) would get Whoopi Goldberg to star alongside "the world's toughest cop," an animatronic puppet of a Tyrannosaurus rex. (A line from a movie poster touting the

conscientious dinosaur literally read, "The world's toughest cop is getting a brand-new partner. He's a real blast from the past.")

The premise of the movie was that an evil DNA expert, Elizar Kane (Armin Mueller-Stahl) had, to all outward appearances, brought dinosaurs back to life with good intentions. In reality, his plan involved destroying the sun and plunging the planet into a new ice age in which he would survive by being frozen on his personal ark. Apparently, this would make him the leader of a post–ice age world. (Although, of course this could never be, given that he destroyed the sun, and suns tend not to magically reignite.)

No explanation was made as to why these newly revived dinosaurs talked or why these traditionally slow-witted animals now would have fully human intellects. There was also no attempt to maintain consistency or even keep the film true to its own logic. Still, if you accepted the basic premise—and were willing to buy that anything can happen in a universe populated with wisecracking animatronic puppet dinosaurs—it would make perfect sense to you that Goldberg's "tough" cop, Katie Coltrane, would have to partner with one of these dinosaurs and attempt to save the world by using a plan so far-fetched, "it just might work."

Goldberg committed to making this film before she won her Oscar for 1990's *Ghost* and did everything in her power to avoid actually making it. Threats of a lawsuit, however, forced her to make the movie and she responded by showing up to read her lines with the zeal of someone sentenced to make PSAs as community service. At times Goldberg was actually out-acted by her very poorly puppeteered prehistoric partner, and seeing this movie ends the debate over whether *Bogus* or *Eddie* represented the least inspired performance of Goldberg, the one-time star of *The Color Purple*.

Despite the ridiculous premise, poor performances, and lousy script, the film still cost $35 million. While $35 million in today's dollars represents the budget of a modest romantic comedy co-starring Hugh Grant, in 1995 it was a significant amount to spend on a cop-buddy film. That made it all the more shocking when New Line decided to forego a theatrical release of the film, instead quietly releasing it direct to video.

By keeping it out of theaters, New Line avoided having the movie be considered one of the biggest box office disasters of all time. Releasing it direct to video also kept the film from being reviewed by newspapers across the country and robbed the nation of a Whoopi Goldberg publicity tour where she would have to tout a film she had only made to avoid a lawsuit.

Goldberg's reluctance to star in the movie proved prescient as it quickly cooled off her career. She immediately followed *Theodore Rex* with the almost equally abysmal *Eddie* (where she coaches the Knicks), *Bogus* (where Gérard Depardieu plays an imaginary French monster), and *The Associate* (where she works for conspicuously white people on Wall Street). Though she appeared in a number of other lousy movies after those three, Goldberg largely moved to television where she starred in a revamped *Hollywood Squares* and a self-titled sitcom where she inexplicably played a soul singer who owned a hotel. She currently appears on *The View* where she seems more successful than during her quickly cancelled syndicated talk show—the cleverly titled *The Whoopi Goldberg Show*.

Theodore Rex did little for the careers of its other major players, as director Jonathan Beutel's filmography literally ends with the film for which he also received a writing credit. Mueller-Stahl faired slightly better, moving onto a career of guest appearances on decent television dramas, including *The X-Files* and *The West Wing*.

Worst Talking-Animal Movies Ever

Howard the Duck. Executive produced by George Lucas before he realized that he should only make movies with *Star Wars* or *Indiana Jones* in the title, *Howard the Duck* was about a duck from another planet who ended up stuck in Cleveland. Based on a comic book, *Howard the Duck* did introduce the martial arts style "Quack Fu," a precursor to Shaquille O'Neal's "Shaq Fu," which went on to become a lousy rap record and video game. Lucas actually spent $2 million for the duck suit, which was only slightly more believable than your average dime-store Halloween costume.

Monkeybone. Another big-budget, box-office bomb, *Monkeybone* paired Brendan Fraser with a monkey who began the story as a comic book character, but came to life after Fraser's character fell into a coma. Highly regarded and distinguished actor John Turturro provides the voice for Monkeybone, a fact he most assuredly leaves off his resume. Whoopi Goldberg appears in the film as a character aptly named Death.

Babe: Pig in the City. This movie sequel wasn't so much wretched as unnecessary. Though the film got some decent reviews, its dark tone and the fact that one talking-pig movie may be cute, but two is redundant, doomed it at the box office. Sadly, this movie proved that there really aren't that many leading roles for talking pigs, and trying to design a plot for one treats the audience to a movie as forced as the *Crocodile Dundee* sequels.

Worst TV Spin-Offs Ever: A Successful Show Does Not Always Mean a Successful Spin-Off

NBC's long-running megahit show *Friends* was built around a group of six somewhat unlikely friends and their love lives, which often involved each other. Even though all six characters were billed as equals, in reality, the show's true leads were usually Jennifer Aniston and David Schwimmer as the "will they or won't they?/why would she date him?" couple Ross and Rachel and the eventual, more plausible couple of Chandler (Matthew Perry) and Monica (Courtney Cox). Lisa Kudrow's dim-witted but loveable Phoebe and Matt

LeBlanc's similarly dim-witted and loveable Joey were more comic relief characters. Sure, they occasionally got lead plot-lines, but usually they were used to add jokes as their characters were less real people than the other four, more traditional sitcom archetypes.

That made Joey a poor choice for a spin-off as he hardly seemed to have the depth of character required to carry his own show. This wasn't Frasier Crane on *Cheers* with an unexplored life as a psychiatrist, this was Newman from *Seinfeld* where some was good, but a lot might be too much.

Much like what happened with *Frasier*, *Joey* involved taking a familiar character and moving him to a new place. Instead of New York where *Friends* took place, *Joey* took place in Los Angeles. And much like Frasier was given a brother and a father we had never heard about on *Cheers*, Joey was given a sister (Drea de Matteo) and a nephew (Paulo Costnazo).

Joey was put into *Friends'* familiar 8:00PM Thursday timeslot by NBC, and expectations were very high. *Friends* had been one of the most popular shows in television history, and its final episode was one of those major TV events that seemingly the entire nation watches. In retrospect, given the cost of securing LeBlanc and the hype surrounding the parent series, the bar for this spin-off was being set impossibly high, and *Joey* was pretty much doomed to failure unless it was very cleverly done, with great writing and a plausible expansion of the simplistic Joey character.

Sadly, none of those things happened, and California Joey, though slightly less dumb and a lot more successful, was mostly still just a guy that women liked who talked about food a lot. Ratings were decent for the first year—not anywhere near what was hoped for, but good enough for a renewal that was likely balanced against the money guaranteed to LeBlanc that the show would be given two years.

NBC had initially given the show a huge push, and the debut episode was watched by nearly nineteen million people. Those numbers quickly decreased through the show's two-year run with *Joey* averaging ten million viewers in its first season, then just over seven in the second. By the time the final episode was broadcast, just over four million people were watching, and NBC actually did not air episodes that had already been shot.

Joey, however, was not the first or even the worst TV spin-off from a massively popular show whose finale was an event that rivaled the Super Bowl in viewership. That honor instead goes to *M*A*S*H* spin-off, *AfterMASH*. This show was doomed because they couldn't get any of the main characters from the parent series to reprise their parts. The public might want to know what Hawkeye did after the war that he hated so much, but Alan Alda wasn't available. The producers of *AfterMASH* couldn't get Hawkeye, B.J., or even Hotlips and Frank Burns, so this ill-fated spin-off stars Colonel Potter, Klinger, and Father Mulcahy as they leave the high-pressure life-or-death stress of the Korean War for the much less dramatic happenings at a veterans hospital.

Of course, without the stress of war and the running gag that Klinger wore a dress to be found crazy so he could get a "section 8" that would send him home, there wasn't much interesting about these characters. Colonel Potter was an interesting character on *M*A*S*H* while he balanced the needs of the army with his decidedly nonmilitary unit, but here, he was just an old guy starring in a sitcom.

Spin-off failure, though, was not just reserved for older characters or side characters as the results were equally as poor when the decision was made to spin-off Scott Baio's Chachi and Erin Moran's Joanie on *Joanie Loves Chachi*. *Happy Days* had already successfully spun-off *Laverne & Shirley* and successfully, albeit less plausibly, *Mork & Mindy*. Given that logic, perhaps this show should have been called *Joanie & Chachi*. Unfortunately, what made these characters interesting was their prolonged mismatched courtship. Making them a couple pretty much ended that and made this show hard to watch.

Even harder to watch was *The Brady Brides*, a sad attempt to revive the original corny magic that was *The Brady Bunch*. It's hard to choose between this mess and the Brady variety hour, but it's impossible to equal the awfulness of a show that somehow manages to have both Marcia and Jan Brady—and their husbands buying a house together. Of course, wacky hijinks ensue, but fortunately, they only ensued for ten episodes.

Perhaps even less plausible than having the Brady sisters move into the same house with their husbands was the idea that a lifeguard could be some sort of mystery-solving detective at night. That was the premise behind *Baywatch Nights*. This show was for the people who thought *Baywatch* had too many sexy women and not enough David Hasselhoff solving mysteries. This series actually made it two seasons, and in season two, they started ripping off *The X-Files* and having Hoff and the gang battle ghosts, vampires, and other paranormal creatures.

SPORTS

Michael Jordan Leaves Basketball for Baseball: No Really, It Wasn't a Gambling Suspension

Despite being the best basketball player in the world at the absolute height of his career, Michael Jordan announced in the fall of 1993 that he would be leaving basketball to attempt to make it as a pro baseball player. Coming off of three straight NBA titles, Jordan decided that he would not go for four but would, instead, try to make himself into a right fielder.

This might make sense if Jordan had been a dual-sport college athlete or someone who had a long tradition as a baseball player.

Instead, he was just a bored million-aire who assumed that since he was really good at one sport, he would probably be pretty good at another.

Since no athlete, no matter how talented, could go from one sport to another without at least a little practice, Jordan was signed by the Chicago White Sox and sent to the Double A Birmingham Barons. At the time, Jordan announced that he had lost his passion for basket-ball. The public did not buy that particular excuse, and to this day, many people assume Jordan's exit from basketball was a secret suspension due to gambling. Those allegations were never proven—though they linger to this day—and as far as history is concerned, Jordan simply left a sport he may well be the greatest to ever play for one where he was not nearly as good as your average high school all-star.

Despite his staggering natural athletic ability, Jordan proved to be a lousy baseball player. Though he practiced ferociously and made impressive progress for someone who didn't play base-ball, Jordan still played like someone who didn't play baseball. Despite his inability to play, Jordan was still one of the most famous people in the world, and his every action drew a media circus. Nearly forty media outlets covered his initial "I'm going to play baseball" press conference, and the Barons were covered on the road as if they were a Major League team rather than an obscure AA team.

During his time in Birmingham, Jordan and hit .202 with 51 RBIs, 30 stolen bases and 114 strikeouts in 127 games. He also took part in the 1994 Arizona Fall League, where he posted a .252 average for the Scottsdale Scorpions. Jordan's baseball career was interrupted by the 1995 baseball strike, which sent "His Airness" back to the basketball court.

Bulls and White Sox owner Jerry Reinsdorf charitably says that he believes that if the strike had not occurred, Jordan would have made the big leagues as a fourth of fifth outfielder. Even if that was true, the greatest basketball player in the world gave up more than a season and likely two championships for the possibility of being a bench player in another sport.

Other Ill-Advised Exits

- **David Caruso leaves *NYPD Blue*.** After one season and four episodes, David Caruso left his hit television program to become a film star. Sadly, that choice did not turn out so well as Caruso's two major films, *Kiss of Death* and *Jade*, both bombed at the box office. Caruso's return to TV in the series *Michael Hayes* also bombed as *NYPD Blue* kept chugging along, ultimately running for twelve seasons. Caruso remained out in the cold—essentially out of the business for eight years—until his ultimate comeback on *CSI Miami.*

- **Michael Ovitz leaves CAA for Disney.** As the founder and leader of the Creative Arts Agency, Michael Ovitz was an enormously powerful agent and one of the most powerful men in Hollywood. That made it quite odd when in 1995—for no obvious reason—he quit CAA to become president of Disney. Though Disney was a large company, it was run by another powerful man who didn't want to share his power, Michael Eisner. At Disney, Ovitz had few responsibilities. He lasted about a year before he was fired by Eisner and largely faded into obscurity.

- **Apple shows Steve Jobs the door.** Though he had created the company and was its symbolic and intellectual leader, Steve Jobs was actually forced out of Apple Computer during a sales slump in 1985. During his exile, Apple continued to struggle, and Jobs went on to lead a little company that would become Pixar—the incredibly successful animation studio that was ultimately sold to Disney for billions. In 1996, Apple realized its mistake and spent nearly $500 million to buy another Jobs's company, NeXT, bringing their iconic leader back into the fold. That, of course, led to the iPod, iPhone, and Apple's complete turnaround—a remarkable comeback that almost didn't happen since Apple nearly went out of business after foolishly pushing its leader aside.

Legendary Coach Jimmy Johnson Endorses Penis-Enhancement Pill: Go Long

Normally a celebrity only endorses products of questionable legitimacy when nobody will hire him for anything else. Kind of the equivalent of appearing at a car show or signing autographs in a high school gym, the dubious product endorsement is usually a money-making tactic of last resort.

That makes me wonder if former college and NFL coach Jimmy Johnson has a gambling problem or if someone has been blackmailing him over something he really does not want to become public. Johnson, who won a national title at Miami and two Super Bowls coaching the Cowboys, hardly seems down on his luck. He currently stars on Fox's NFL pregame show (probably a seven-figure gig for one day of work a week less than half the year), and he would be an in-demand, highly paid corporate speaker. And of course, don't forget that Johnson was one of the highest paid coaches in the game

during his stint with the Cowboys and his later, less-successful gig with the Dolphins. Plus, if he needs money, he would likely be an in-demand coach at $5–$7 million per year or could get one of those easy, lucrative, team president gigs like Mike Holmgren has with the Cleveland Browns that pays millions per year.

With all of those financial options available to him, one has to question why Johnson instead chose to endorse ExtenZe, an extremely dubious "male enhancement" pill touted in late-night television commercials. ExteZe isn't Viagra, Cialis, or any other legitimate drug prescribed by a doctor or approved by the FDA. Instead, it's one of those "it couldn't possibly work, but I'll try it anyway" pills found on the checkout counter at less-reputable convenience stores.

Johnson not only endorses the product, he seems to actually truly support it as in his multiple commercials for the pill, he seems to be enjoying himself. Unlike, say, Mr. T in the Flavor Wave Oven infomercial, where he looks like he's a hostage, Johnson seems quite taken with the idea that this pill will make his penis bigger (though he has to know it won't). In one ad, Johnson delivers the line, "Most men want to perform the best they can in just about everything. Isn't that why we buy the biggest and best of everything?" He ends the ad, with the cringe-inducing tagline, "Go long with ExtenZe. I do."

Before signing on with ExtenZe, Johnson had to know of its less-than-stellar reputation as in 2006, according to the *Los Angeles Times*, ExtenZe agreed to pay the Orange County, California district attorney's office $300,000 in civil penalties for unfair business practices and false advertising. At the time of that lawsuit, Susan Kang Schroeder of the DA's office said the company could not back up its claim that the pills caused users' penises to grow 27 percent.

Dr. Ira Sharlip, a spokesman for the American Urological Association, put it even more clearly to *Newsday*, saying, "There is no such thing as a penis pill that works. These are all things that are sold for profit. There's no science or substance behind them."

Short of major financial problems, one would have to wonder why a still-working former NFL coach would choose to endorse a product whose validity has been publicly questioned and whose use, even if it did work, would be embarrassing to admit you need publicly. Endorsing ExtenZe is the equivalent of going on TV and saying, "I have a small penis," not usually something most men are willing to do.

Questionable Celebrity Endorsements

Mr. T: The Flavor Wave Oven. First the *A-Team* movie uses someone else as B. A. Baracus, and then Mr. T has to resort to endorsing this odd cooking system. It's not so much T's presence in the commercial as it is the lines he is forced to deliver. It's one thing to make him say versions of his own signature lines like "I pity the fool, who don't try this salmon," but it's truly miserable when T has to deliver lines that weren't even his from *The A-Team*. It also appears that T is wearing a press-on Mohawk in these ads, and he looks as happy to be there as Woody Allen would be at a Klan meeting.

Pope Leo and Cocaine Wine. In the 1880s, Pope Leo XIII, Queen Victoria, and Pope Saint Pius X praised Vin Mariani, a popular drink made from Bordeaux wine laced with cocaine. Though cocaine-laced wine may not be the worst thing ever endorsed by a pope, it was a pretty questionable move. Pope Leo XIII even awarded a gold medal to the drink and appeared in a poster endorsing it. The ad stated, "His Holiness the Pope writes that he has fully appreciated the beneficent effects of this Tonic Wine and has forwarded to Mr. Mariani as a token of his gratitude a gold medal bearing his august effigy."

Hulk Hogan, Troy Aikman, and Rent-A-Center. The Hulkster's presence in this ad makes sense. He lost a ton of money in the divorce, "brother," self-tanner, and bandanas cost some serious dough; but Aikman's presence in these commercials seems odd. Like Jimmy Johnson, Aikman not only has a thriving TV career, but he made over $100 million in his playing career. While Hulk might have to be here, you would think Aikman could turn down the money offered to trick poor people into dramatically overpaying for TVs, couches, and other household items offered by Rent-A-Center on "rent-to-own" plans.

Mikhail Gorbachev pitches Pizza Hut. From the leader of one of the most powerful countries in the world to a commercial endorsing one of America's crappy pizza brands, former Soviet President Mikhail Gorbachev fell fast and hard. As if losing the Cold War wasn't bad enough, the once-powerful leader was reduced to taking a job the average sitcom star would scoff at. At least this deal did not lead to a borscht pizza or Pizza Hut offering fountain vodka.

Major League Baseball Pushes the Sammy Sosa and Mark McGwire Home Run Chase: Please Ignore Their Giant Heads

28

Heading into the 1998 season, Major League Baseball had fallen upon hard times. The league had still not recovered from the labor dispute that led to the cancellation of the 1994 World Series, and the public seemed disenchanted with what had once been "America's national pastime." Football was more violent—plus it had both the betting and the fantasy crowds—and basketball had captured hearts and minds of the youth audience. Baseball, with its slower pace and low scores, it was starting to seem, was a product of a bygone

era—something that old men watched as they intermittently nodded off in front of the TV.

Enter Mark McGwire and Sammy Sosa. One was a redheaded hulk of a man, likeable but quiet, a classic slugger who harkened back to the baseball players of old. The other was an outgoing Dominican who spoke broken English and flashed his charming smile. They seemed like superheroes, and in 1998, the two would race to break what was considered an almost unbreakable record—Roger Maris's 61 home runs.

Because McGwire and Sosa were each affable in their own way, the public entirely bought into the race for 61. Baseball officials and media—who had to have their suspicions—not only fueled the fire, they actually made excuses for the two sluggers. Stories about juiced balls and thin pitching rotations abounded, but nobody suggested that the homeruns were flying because of juiced players and thin drug policies.

Never mind that McGwire and Sosa (McGwire especially) looked as if they were a pair of tattered green pants away from being the Incredible Hulk, nobody ever mentioned steroids. In 1998, you could get steroids in pretty much any gym in America, but nobody raised the issue because the two hitters seemed like such nice fellows, and Sosa made endearing pointing gestures on the field.

As the battle went late into the season, McGwire's Cardinals actually met Sosa's Cubs, and a lovefest ensued. As McGwire launched the first pitch, he saw just barely out of the stadium—breaking the record—he circled the bases, and hugged

every one of the Cubs' infielders. After the Cards met McGwire at home plate, Sosa came in from his position in right field to congratulate McGwire. Everybody loved everybody, and nobody even hinted at the idea that anyone was cheating.

And of course, like someone who robs a jewelry store and wears a new diamond ring to work the next day, McGwire could not resist going on tour to show what a fabulous guy he was. After breaking the record, McGwire then proceeded to visit with Maris's children.

As the years went by and baseball started to sort of pretend it wanted to clean itself up and get rid of steroids, suspicions began to pile up. Of course, suspicions were only that until a player either got caught in a test or got investigated by the government. Even players who tested positive had a fairly easy way out as the public has been very forgiving of players that simply own what

they did. Andy Pettitte admitted his steroid use and went on to play a few more successful seasons. Roger Clemens denied his, and he will likely end up in jail.

Still, despite all the circumstantial evidence, the public wanted to believe that the home run chase had been legit. We promised not to look too hard or ask too many questions, and McGwire and Sosa would continue to be heroes—perhaps not the heroes they were, but certainly not the villains they would ultimately become.

This public-player pact lasted until 2005 when the busy-bodies in Congress decided they needed to clean up baseball. Why Congress would choose baseball from all of the problems facing the country nobody knows, but baseball it was, and Mark McGwire was called to testify.

Around this time, Sosa, who had always spoken English in a semicomedic fashion, forgot the language, and began communicating only through carefully worded statements released by his public-relations people. The once-affable slugger turned into a silent figure who never quite confirmed or denied his drug use.

McGwire, on the other hand, went to Congress and denied everything. This might have been plausible if the player, only four years into retirement, had not shown up looking like a skinnier version of Ron Howard from *Happy Days*. Once a towering He-Man, McGwire sat before Congress a shadow of his former self, a frail old man who acknowledged that steroids were a problem in baseball but denied ever having done them himself.

In denying the obvious, McGwire broke his and Sosa's tenuous pact with the public, casting aspersions on not only the 1998 home run chase, but the entire group of '90s home run hitters. Suddenly, every home run was cast into doubt, and any power hitter with even the vaguest hint of steroids scandal became an outcast.

Once heralded as saviors of the sport, McGwire and Sosa are now symbols of everything that has gone wrong with baseball. Instead of making the Hall of Fame, both will be lucky to get enough votes to stay on the ballot. Of course, while baseball was promoting these two as superheroes, officials almost certainly knew that they were most likely taking steroids, but it was clearly decided that the short-term gain was worth the long-term loss. Now, most '80s and '90s baseball records have the credibility of pro wrestling, or worse, competitive cycling.

29

The XFL: Pro Football Plus Pro Wrestling Equals Ratings Disaster

New sports leagues have a success rate well below that of celebrity marriages, and most have even less longevity. In 2001, when wrestling promoter Vince McMahon and NBC (the then-network of *Inside Schwartz* and *Emeril*) launched the XFL, a new football league, the sports landscape already contained the corpses of countless failures. These include, but are not limited to, the United States Football League, the World Football League (not to be confused with the World

League of American Football), the World Hockey Association, countless indoor soccer leagues, a variety of women's basketball outfits, and the American expansion arm of the Canadian Football League.

Clearly, starting a sports league at all has historically been a bad idea. But taking on the National Football League, an organization that had systematically crushed its competition, seemed especially foolhardy. Still, in February 2000, fresh off losing its package of NFL games, NBC decided to back McMahon in the creation of a new football league.

McMahon, not only the owner and promoter of the World Wrestling Federation (now World Wrestling Entertainment), but also an active wrestling character, served as the face of the joint venture with NBC and held a February 2, 2000, press conference. Much like he did in his role as the evil billionaire chairman of the WWF, McMahon delivered an over-the-top wrestling promo that pushed the bounds of good taste.

The fifty-something multimillionaire with a weirdly jacked-up upper body promised the new league would be more violent than the NFL. He announced that there would be no touchbacks, more hitting, and fewer rules designed to keep the players safe. He also promised that cameras would be every-where and that players, coaches, cheerleaders, sidelines, and locker rooms would be wired for sound. Players would all make the same salaries, with winning teams sharing in a bonus pool, and the eventual champion sharing in an even bigger pool.

The new league would also have even more ridiculous rule changes, including scrapping the opening coin toss in favor of a violent fifteen-yard dash for a ball, which would determine

which team would get the first possession. Extra points were also dropped in favor of mandatory two-point conversions. The league also tried to allow defensive backs to hit wide receivers at will, but that rule was switched back to the NFL's rule in week four because all the interference due to hitting made passing nearly impossible.

The league's credibility was doubted from week one. Apparently, being the owner of a fake sport did not exactly qualify someone to own a real sport in the eyes of many fans. And while the on-the-field product looked real, it was hard for fans to get past the idea that at any moment, one player might hit another with a steel chair.

The XFL also introduced the idea that players ought to put sayings on their jerseys instead of their names. Like a league-sanctioned version of Jim McMahon's rule-flaunting headbands, the most famous instance of this new wrinkle was Rod "He Hate Me" Smart's choice to put "They Hate Me" on his shirt. Since "They Hate Me" wouldn't fit, "He Hate Me" became the catch-phrase of choice.

Still, opening-week ratings were high, which NBC and McMahon mistook as fan interest instead of people tuning in to see just how big a mess the XFL would be. By week three, the numbers had plummeted, and the league was reduced to the promotion of halftime stunts including "going inside the cheerleaders' locker rooms."

Though the first season did ultimately finish with the "Million Dollar Game" championship—so-called because the winning team split $1 million—it was quickly canceled before season two. NBC and McMahon lost an estimated $70 million on the league, and McMahon lost any chance he may have ever had of creating a successful venture outside the wrestling business.

Worst Sports Leagues Ever

Isaiah Thomas buys the CBA. Formed in 1946, the Continental Basketball Association operated successfully until 1999, when it was purchased by a group led by former NBA great Isaiah Thomas. Though Thomas promised to lead the league to greater heights, he ultimately abandoned it to take a job coaching the Indiana Pacers, leading to the CBA's eventual demise in 2001.

Vince McMahon creates World Bodybuilding Federation. This was McMahon's attempt to duplicate the success he had with wrestling by giving pro bodybuilders outrageous characters to play. Unfortunately, while his wrestling characters used their outrageousness to get fans excited about their eventual physical confrontations, the men of the WBF didn't fight; they simply stood and posed.

Two women's basketball leagues started at the same time. The ongoing but money-losing WNBA and the American Basketball League (ABL) both began in 1997. Somehow, the founders of the ABL thought it was a good idea to continue their underfunded concept in the face of competition from a rival league supported by the NBA. Despite the fact that America had never shown it could support one, let alone two women's leagues, both competitors somehow saw the light of day.

USFL attempts to take on the NFL. By playing in the spring and spending huge money on famous players like Doug Flutie and Herschel Walker, this upstart league, formed in 1983, hoped to take on its more established rival. At first the splashy moves (which included signing players away from the NFL) got the USFL attention, but the high cost of competing with the National Football League quickly became too much even for deep-pocketed owners such as Donald Trump. When the league folded in 1985, it sued the NFL for $1.5 billion and won, but a judge ordered damages in the amount of $3.76 million, which were not quite enough to bring the league back or recoup its many losses.

The WUSA forms. Founded based on the idea that interest in the 1999 Women's World Cup translated to interest in a full-time women's soccer league in the United States, this league was launched in 2000 before collapsing three years later. In retrospect, launching a full-time soccer league due to interest in the World Cup would be like creating a full-time luge league after the Winter Olympics.

CFL expands in the United States. Perhaps unaware of the failure of the USFL, the long-running Canadian Football League decided to add teams in the United States in 1993. Poor attendance and confusion over the bizarre rules, which included three down series and having twelve players on the field at the same time led to the U.S. division of the league closing in 1995.

Minnesota Vikings Trade Everything for Herschel Walker: Mortgaging Your Future for a Star's Last Hurrah

30

L
ike bragging that you slept with Elizabeth Taylor in 2005, instead of 1980, the Minnesota Vikings traded away their future for the rights to a nearly-finished Herschel Walker. To understand the true foolishness of the Vikings' actions, one must realize that NFL running backs—even ones in superb condition as Walker famously was—have a very short prime. Most running backs burn out in three to four years, and even elite runners rarely last more than six as top players.

Before being traded to the Vikings, Walker had already logged many years as a pro, including a less-than-luxurious three-year stint in the USFL. Walker then played for Dallas in the 1986–1989 seasons before being sent to Minnesota. That meant that by the time Walker came to his new team, he had already logged six seasons as a top running back. It was not unreasonable to expect that he still had some tread left on the tires, but nobody would expect him to remain a top player for more than two or three more years.

That did not stop the Vikings from giving Dallas five servicable players and six draft picks, including two first round and two second round selections. These picks ultimately turned into which led to Emmitt Smith, Russell Maryland, Kevin Smith, and Darren Woodson—three perennial Pro Bowl players and one Hall-of-Famer.

To say Walker never led the Vikings to the heights he was expected to would be putting it mildly. Though he had made the Pro Bowl in two of the previous three seasons before becoming a Viking, Walker would never rush for one thousand yards in his two years with the team.

Dallas, of course, profited mightily from the deal acquiring much of the core of its eventual championship teams. The Cowboys even reacquired Walker for the 1996 and 1997 seasons where he served as sort of a utility player filling a variety of roles on offense, defense, and special teams. Currently, Walker is dabbling in mixed martial arts, the Dallas Cowboys have three Super Bowl wins since "the Trade," and Minnesota continues to search for its first world title since before the NFL and AFL merged.

Monday Night Football Hires Dennis Miller: Comedian Makes Games Not So Funny

Despite the National Football League being the most popular sports league in the United States and ABC being one of the biggest, most successful sports network in the country (the biggest when you add in that they own ESPN), ABC could not resist tampering with America's most popular sport. Put more directly, even though viewers already love the NFL the way it is, ABC executives could not help themselves when it came to trying to make the game even more popular. But when all the sports fans already like you, the only way to become more popular is to try to reach out to nonsports fans.

Entertaining nonsports fans has long been the reason the Olympics garner so much viewership. Sure, sometimes the actual events offer compelling storylines, but if they don't, the networks are more than happy to manufacture some. Curling might be the most boring sport in history—it's essentially people standing over a giant puck while sweeping the ice with a broom—but add in a features package about how Canada's team captain had to grow up being bullied for his lisp (to ratchet up the drama he would invariably be from Saskatoon, Saskatchewa) and you have instant drama.

Since the players did not change from week to week, ABC (which for countless years owned the popular *Monday Night Football* package) could not reach casual fans with player profiles or other personality features. Instead, the only way to bring in nonsports fans would be to introduce nonsports entertainment into the broadcast booth. They decided to do this by adding a comedian to the broadcast team—essentially to add some laughs and broaden the audience.

In theory, this idea made sense. A comedian jumping in with this occasional might make the prime-time games more palatable for the casual-viewing audience as long as the jokes were kept in the background and didn't overrun the reason most of the audience had tuned it. The idea would have made even more sense if ABC had hired a mainstream comedian with mass appeal. Instead, they hired Dennis Miller.

Since he entered the public consciousness as the host of the "Weekend Update" segment on *Saturday Night Live*, Miller had been considered a cerebral comedian. Though that act brought him a loyal following, and it worked well as a counterbalance to *SNL*'s less-intelligent sketch offerings, it did not always play well on a wide stage. That was proven when Miller's attempt at a late-night talk show failed as did a number of other attempts to turn the comedian into a television star.

As a comedian, Miller did hip intelligent material peppered with references that some of the audience did not always get. As a *Monday Night Football* commentator, Miller dropped the intelligent funny material and mostly made references that nobody got. You would think ABC was paying Miller by the obscure joke or that he had some elaborate bet with a billionaire who paid him huge sums to mention more and more ridiculous things with every passing game. Miller's act was so hard to follow that Al Michaels (play-by-play) and Dan Fouts (traditional color commentator) mostly ignored him making the hard-to-follow jokes go over like lead balloons.

Miller was unpopular from that start, and his refusal to tell any jokes that most of the country could actually laugh at did little to make him more popular. Instead, websites popped up that explained the comedian's references ,and Miller became the symbol for obnoxious highbrow entertainers who have no actual interest in entertaining their audience. In the end, ABC killed the Dennis Miller experiment after two years, though ESPN (by then owned by ABC and managing their sports division) would repeat the mistake by putting funny columnist and radio host Tony Kornheiser in the *Monday Night Football* booth. Though Kornheiser was less obscure than Miller, he was also not a comedian and not nearly as capable at making one-liners. Kornheiser can be quite funny in print, and his *Pardon the Interruption* pioneered a new kind of entertaining sports commentary, but his act did not play well as part of a three-man broadcast booth.

ESPN Hires Rush Limbaugh

Though they were smart enough to keep him out of the broadcast booth, ESPN once again tried to expand its audience for NFL football by making right-wing talk show host Rush Limbaugh a commentator on its Sunday afternoon *NFL Countdown* pregame show. Limbaugh, who makes his living saying controversial things, only made it a few weeks when he made the following comments about then Philadelphia Eagles quarterback Donavon McNabb.

"I think what we've had here is a little social concern in the NFL. The media has been very desirous that a black quarterback do well. There is a little hope invested in McNabb, and he got a lot of credit for the performance of this team that he didn't deserve. The defense carried this team."

Whether his comments were true, or at least defensible, proved to be irrelevant as it were if you're Rush Limbaugh, you cannot go on an NFL pregame show and imply that the media wants a black quarterback too well even if he's not really that good. The blowback was tremendous and immediate as activist groups and African-American groups quickly called for Limbaugh to be fired. The talk show host did not allow ESPN that pleasure, however, as he resigned the following Wednesday hopefully, forever ending the practice of putting nonsports people into sports broadcasting roles.

32

The Trailblazers Choose Sam Bowie over Michael Jordan: It Seemed Like a Good Idea at the Time

Michael Jordan is almost unanimously regarded as the greatest basketball player who ever lived. Sam Bowie is not. An entirely unremarkable player who, when healthy, had a decent albeit unspectacular career, Bowie was supposed to be better than he was, but recurring leg injuries caused him to miss lots of games and ultimately mar his career. Had he not been the player picked before the greatest player to ever play the game, Bowie's selection in 1984 would have been considered mildly disappointing. Instead, it has gone down as one of the biggest—if not the actual biggest—blunders in sports.

People actually forget that neither Bowie nor Jordan was the first pick in the 1984 National Basketball Association draft. That honor instead went to Hakeem Olajuwon, a great player who was still no Jordan. Still, Olajuwon ultimately won two NBA titles in back-to-back years as a member of the Houston Rockets. Of course, those two titles happened in years when Jordan was not playing basketball but was instead trolling the minor leagues as a baseball player. Had Olajuwon not won those titles, his being picked over Jordan would be questioned, certainly not as much as Bowie's selection was, but on a pretty grand level.

Though history has rendered the selection of Bowie over Jordan as one of the worst draft-day choices in history, it was not quite that cut-and-dried on draft day in 1984. Portland, unlike most teams selecting number two, was not a bottom-tier team. Instead, they had obtained the second pick in the draft through a trade, and they were not looking at rebuilding their franchise. Instead, they were looking at adding a piece that was ready to play in the NBA that might help put their team over the top.

Portland also needed a center, which Bowie was and Jordan, of course, was not. Their main divisional rival was the Los Angeles Lakers, which had the dominating presence of Kareem Abdul-Jabbar. The Trailblazers also had Mychal Thompson, a strong forward who lacked the bulk to be a center. If the team could add a powerful, bulky center, then Thompson could play his game, theoretically making the whole team stronger. So while everyone knew Jordan had a bigger upside than Bowie, he was viewed as raw potential and not a ready-made NBA player who would fill the Blazers' biggest need. Portland also had strong guards in all-star Jim Paxson and future superstar Clyde Drexler. In addition the team had the top-notch scorer Kiki Vandeweghe as their small forward. Basically, Portland, on paper, did not need any more scoring. The team needed a big body at center.

Because of that, the Portland Trailblazers overlooked Jordan's tremendous upside and picked Bowie over Jordan. Had Bowie stayed healthy, he may very well have led the Blazers—a more complete team—over Jordan's Bulls in the NBA finals. Instead, Jordan went on to win six titles, and Bowie became the answer to a trivia question.

Worst Draft Picks Ever

Seattle Seahawks pick Rick Mirer second in the 1994 draft. Though Mirer went on to a decent career as a journeyman backup, the most stunning part of his being picked second in the 1994 draft was that it was touch and go that he might be picked first by the New England Patriots. In New England, and across the nation, Drew Bledsoe versus Mirer was a legitimate discussion. And while Bledsoe's career was derailed and stopped just short of the Hall of Fame by the emergence of Tom Brady, he did get his team to a Super Bowl and won the AFC championship game when Brady went down with an injury during the Patriots' first Super Bowl–winning season. Mirer never led Seattle much of anywhere, and while he got lots of chances, he was a career backup who held on for a long time because he looked like a quarterback and was an intelligent albeit mostly unsuccessful player.

Ottawa Senators select Alexandre Daigle first in 1993. Billed as the next Mario Lemeiux. Daigle never panned out as an NHL player bouncing between teams and stints in the minors, never putting up more than fifty-one points in the season. Daigle's failure was magnified by how incredibly hyped his arrival was, but he was still a colossal failure.

New York Yankees pick Brien Taylor first in 1991. Not only was Taylor picked first by the Yankees, he received a then-record $1.55 million signing bonus—about $1 million more than previous record. Taylor never played a game for the Yankees as he blew out his arm in an off-field fight before rising out of the low minors.

St. Louis Rams take Lawrence Phillips sixth in 1996: Sometimes, college players with off-field troubles overcome them and go on to great NFL careers. That was not the case for Phillips who ran for 1,400 yard in three years with the Rams. Eddie George, a likely Hall of Fame running back, went thirteenth to the Oilers in this same draft.

The Bowl Champion Series: Taking a Bad System and Making It Worse

ivision I college football has never done a very good job in crowning its champion. The system has always relied on the inexact science of coaches' polls, writers' polls and other somewhat arbitrary methods of deciding who the National Champion was. For years, there were four major bowl games (The Fiesta Bowl, The Sugar Bowl, The Cotton Bowl and The Rose Bowl). These varied throughout the years as sometimes one became less important and sometimes another snuck in, but

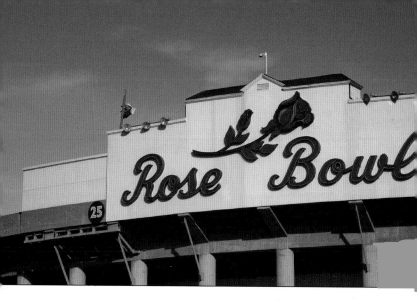

there was a group of major bowls which all had ties to the most powerful conferences.

Those conference ties created the first set of problems as certain conference champions had to play in certain bowl games, it was nearly impossible to guarantee that the top two teams in the nation would play in a national title game. Instead the number one team might play the number six team and the number two team might play the number three team. If both number one and number two won, it would not be clear which was actually better and who should be declared the Nation Champion.

To say this has caused confusion throughout the years would be putting it mildly. In many seasons we had split national champions with the AP poll supporting one team and the coaches' poll another. Never mind that almost nobody voting in either poll actually saw most of the regular season, these votes decided who the champion was, not any sort of actual game. In some years, you even had three or four teams claiming a piece of the National Championship and still others who considered themselves the uncrowned title holders.

As important as clearly crowning a National Champion was the idea that teams would have something to play for. Under the old system, once a major power lost, it would be unlikely that they would have any chance of climbing back into the title picture. And, if a team from a less-powerful, "mid-major," conference went undefeated, they would have no shot at playing for a National Championship. Instead, they would play in one of the dozens of relatively irrelevant bowl games that might be popular revenue sources for the NCAA but were largely meaningless in the process of determining who really had the best football team.

Fans hated this system and clamored for a playoff. Sure, they argued about whether it should be eight teams or 16, but fans wanted a tournament to decide which team actually was the best in the nation—exactly like we have in every professional sport.

Instead, the NCAA gave the fans a mild tweak on the current system. There would be no playoffs and most of the bowls would stay exactly as they were, but one bowl would be played last and that bowl would match up the top two teams in the nation. Called the Bowl Championship Series (BCS), this new system ignored the idea that it was next-to-impossible most seasons to figure out which teams should be ranked in the top two spots.

Should an undefeated team in a lesser conference get a shot? What about a one loss team whose loss came early, on the road and against another powerhouse teams? How do you decide in years where there are multiple one loss teams who played similar schedules?

Instead of solving the problem, the BCS just changed it slightly. It would be like if your house were flooded with sewage and instead of cleaning up you bought an air freshener. The BCS does succeed in matching up the top two teams as voted by the various polls, but that has hardly cut down on the debate as to who the actual National Champion is.

The fans want a playoff with some teams getting in due to winning their conferences and other getting at-large bids based on their record and strength of schedule. Instead, the NCAA gives them more silliness in which writers and coaches casting ballots decided who the best football team is. That would be like picking the country's best burger by looking at pictures.

34

The LeBron James Decision: He Spits on His People, Takes His "Talents to South Beach"

For the first seven years of his career, LeBron James got to play in Cleveland in front of his hometown fans. James had grown up in Akron, Ohio and by blind luck, he ended up being drafted by the Cleveland Cavaliers—a beleaguered franchise in a city full of equally woeful teams. Clevelanders—though they are legendarily loyal to their sports teams—have had precious little to cheer about. The Indians have mostly been terrible (even inspiring the *Major League* movies about the fantastical possibility that the Indians actually won.

The city had even suffered the indignity of having its beloved NFL franchise leave for Baltimore. Despite the rabid "dog pound" which supported the team passionately, owner Art Modell needed money and he split for Baltimore. Though the league ultimately brought a new Browns team to Cleveland, that franchise has been terrible for its entire existence, running through head coaches and starting quarterbacks at an alarming rate.

The Cavaliers had also mostly been losers, but all that changed when hometown superstar, "King" LeBron James ended up property of his hometown team. In an instant, the franchise went from also-ran to perennial title contender. James had very little talent around him during his first few seasons, but he instantly made the team a winner, restoring pride in his home state and becoming the symbol of Cleveland 's—and the rest of Ohio's—rebirth. James wasn't just a superstar athlete, he was a local boy winning in front of his people—people that loved and supported him in a way that few athletes enjoyed. Most fans have become jaded. They realize that players play for money and that they may wear a city's name on their jersey, but they have no actual loyalty to that team or those fans.

James, though, people wanted to believe was different. He was not merely an athlete drafted by a team in Ohio who had to live there, he was actually from Akron, Ohio and he—the fans desperately wanted to believe—was actually loyal because he had grown up with the disappointment of being a Cleveland fan. LeBron was not merely a basketball player, he was the savior bringing pride and a chance to win to his community.

In his seven years the Cavaliers struggled to get supporting players to play alongside James. Though they sought the advice of their young superstar and made many moves that he had suggested, the team never quite got over the hump. James did prove himself a true superstar by leading the team to the 2007 NBA Finals, where they lost in somewhat embarrassing fashion, being swept by the San Antonio Spurs. Still, the team had made the Finals and the fans of Cleveland believed that their young superstar would ultimately lead them to the promised land even if he had to do it with a supporting cast of cast-offs and role players.

A roadblock remained though as James' contract was up following the 2009 season. Cleveland's fans, though, were not worried as not only was James a hometown hero who would—they believed—never let down "his" people, but the Cavaliers could actually pay him more money than any other team. Every factor pointed to the Cavs resigning their superstar, but everyone had overlooked that James was a spoiled millionaire who had never faced any real adversity once people realized how good he was with a basketball in his hands.

Cleveland fans had heard the New York rumors, they had heard the Chicago whispers and they even knew that Miami would make a bid for James' services. They had been convinced that their hero would never betray them, but they had to be a little nervous when he announced that he was going to announce his "decision" in an hour-long ESPN program (pompously named *The Decision*). James might leave, fans thought, but he would never go on TV and rub it in Cleveland's face. Sure, he was going to make his fans sweat—maybe to send a message to management about getting him some more talented team-mates—but they believed he would never go on TV and say he was going elsewhere.

But that was exactly what "King" James did. He went on TV and said, to his handpicked interviewer, that he was "taking his talents to South Beach." In that one simple sentence he compounded the agony for Cleveland's long-suffering fans and while they lay on the ground bleeding, he grabbed the knife and twisted.

The long-suffering sports fans who fell victim to "The Drive," "The Fumble," "The Shot," the loss of the Browns, the sad performance of the Browns since their return and years of futility from the Indians had been crushed again by one of their own LeBron James. They deserved for their hometown hero to go on ESPN and say, "I know it's going to be hard, but this is my home, these are my people and I'm going to work as hard as I can to bring a title to Cleveland."

Instead, they were blindsided and humiliated by one of their own on national television.

James had promised to win a title for Cleveland. He not only came up short in that quest, he didn't actually seem to care very much as he let opportunity slip away the last two years.

Had James stayed in Cleveland and won even one title, he would go down as an immortal. Winning in a city that has historically loses means more to the fans in that city and in the history books. Even without winning a championship, had James stayed a Cavalier, he would have remained a lifelong icon in the place he has always lived to the people who have always supported him. Instead, he chose to betray those fans by not just leaving the team, but by humiliating the Cavaliers on the way out the door.

Lebron James did the equivalent of breaking up with his girlfriend by announcing it on stage at a pep rally the day before the prom. With the words "I'm taking my talents to South Beach," James kicked his hometown fans in the teeth. Instead of taking the hard road and trying to bring Cleveland the title he had promised them, the young superstar turned his back on people who perhaps foolishly had held him up as their sports savior.

James might win in Miami, but stacking the deck with superstars and winning a title as Dwayne Wade's Scottie Pippen does not make you an all-time great. "The King" had a chance to rule, a chance to matter in his community like few athletes do. Instead, he gets to hang out with his buddies in South Beach while Cleveland burns his image in effigy.

35

Disco Demolition Night: Cheap Beer and Destruction May Not Mix

Despite its brief, but enormous, popularity, disco music had its fair share of enemies. Chief amongst those might be sports fans—at least male sports fans—who viewed disco, with its flamboyant outfits, spinning lights and less than macho imagery as something less than manly. By the late 1970s a strong anti-disco movement had taken hold and one major league baseball team thought its marketing people had come up with a brilliant way to capitalize on that sentiment.

Disco Demolition Night actually grew out of an anti-disco movement fed by Chicago Disc Jockey Steve Dahl, who had lost his job when the station he worked for switched from rock music to an all-disco format. Dahl eventually got himself hired at another rock station where he used the publicity surrounding his firing and the growing disco backlash to launch an anti-disco crusade. This mostly included mocking the music with his on-air partner, but his crusade also featured the parody "Do You Think I'm Disco," which of course was making fun of Rod Stewart's hit, "Do You Think I'm Sexy."

The stage was was set for the infamous doubleheader that would include Disco Demolition Night when a game between the White Sox and the Detroit Tigers was rained out and scheduled to be made up in a doubleheader about a month later. Dahl, working with Mike Veeck, the son of then-White Sox owner Bill Veeck, as well as various promotion and marketing people from the radio station and the team came up with the idea that would go so disastrously wrong. Fans would pay only $.98 to get into the game as long as they brought along their unwanted disco music. The records would then be collected and put in a huge crate in center field, where Dahl would quite literally blow them up.

Expectations were not high for this promotion and White Sox management expected less than 15,000 people, which would be about double what the team attracted for a usual weeknight game. Unfortunately, approximately 90,000 people showed up disco records in hand. This was not only a better crowd than anticipated, but it was around twice as many people as the stadium held. Not to be deterred, thousands of fans who had been denied admission to the ballpark decided to scale the walls and enter anyway.

Not only were more fans than expected jammed into the stadium, which was filled well over capacity, there were also too many records for the crate in center field. This left thousands of fans in the stands carrying records. Some of these fans had been drinking and the scent of marijuana was so prevalent that the announcers calling the game actually commented on it. And, perhaps, some of the crowd was more interested in the promotion than in the actual game as records were being tossed around the stadium like Frisbees injuring fans, but stopping short of a full-scale riot.

As the first game ended (Chicago lost) Dahl, dressed in an army outfit complete with a helmet entered the field to lead the crowd in chants of "disco sucks." After the requisite countdown, he hit the button that triggered the explosives and then, all hell broke loose. As the crate exploded, it ripped a huge hole in the outfield and small fires began burning. The fans—maybe powered more by their hatred of disco than their love of the White Sox—then began storming the field. The rioting mob lit more fires, destroyed a batting cage and stole pieces of the field itself. Banners were burned and the destruction was pretty much aimless until police began chasing people of the field. It took police in riot gear to regain order and 39 people were arrested.

The second game was not played due to the condition of the field, but even if the field had been fixable, Detroit's manager, the legendary Sparky Anderson, refused to allow his team back on the field anyway due to concerns for their safety. Ultimately, Major League Baseball declared the game a forfeit and awarded the victory to the Tigers.

Ten Cent Beer Night

Sports fans tend to get drunk and rowdy at a regular game which makes one wonder what the Cleveland Indians were thinking on June 4, 1974 when they offered fans as many beers as they could drink for a dime. This, of course, was a stupendously bad idea as usually the only thing stopping fans from drinking themselves blind was the famously high cost of buying beers at the ballpark.

As the game wore on, the crowd became more and more drunk. This made it increasingly difficult for the umpires to maintain order. Multiple instances of

streakers and flashers as well as multiple moonings, not to mention the fighting in the stands, ultimately forced umpires to call off the game. Unfortunately, before the game could be called, large numbers of fans who had armed themselves with whatever was available (bats, chairs, beer bottles and more) started to destroy the stadium. When this spilled over onto the actual field, the game was cancelled. The bases were stolen (and never found) and significant damage was done to the stadium.

MEDIA &
POLITICS

36

Politically Getting Ahead of Yourself: Perhaps That Mission Wasn't Exactly Accomplished

Politicians love to make promises and they love to tell us how successful they are in delivering on those promises. Usually this involves standing up at a podium and bragging about how many jobs they have created and how fabulous the economy has become. Of course, while these speeches are going on many of us are sitting at home unemployed, not exactly feeling the benefits of this so-called new, improved economy.

Whether it's touting their success with the economy or telling us the many ways their actions have benefitted us, politicians love to speak before we can accurately judge the veracity of their statements. It's easy to stand before the American people and tell us what you have done. It's infinitely harder to actually show us and, sometimes, though the politician tells us he did a good job or succeeded in meeting his goals, the truth turns out to be, well, less so.

Perhaps the most famous example of a politician speaking too soon was on May 1, 2003, when then president George W. Bush stood on the deck of the USS Abraham Lincoln in front of a giant banner that declared "mission accomplished." The mission which had supposedly been accomplished was the successful conclusion of the war in Iraq. In his speech Bush talked about how major combat operations had come to an end and the need for troops would soon be gone. The war was over, he more or less said—we just had to clean up some guerilla operations by some rowdy Iraqis and we could bring our boys home, content in the knowledge that we had won the war bringing the Iraqi people the freedom the so richly desirer and deserved. Sure, there never were any actual weapons of mass destruction, but 'Old Georgie had done all right anyway.

That would make a lot of sense if the war in Iraq had ended anytime in say the next few months. Unfortunately for the president, a man somewhat famous for putting his foot into his mouth and saying dumb things, the war did not end quite that quickly. In fact, the war in Iraq did not end during Bush's presidency, which continued for another whole term. And, despite

Bush declaring that major combat operations had come to an end, the vast majority of American casualties actually occurred after the "mission accomplished" speech.

Though nobody knew just how preposterous declaring that the war was over in May of 2003, Bush's speech was met with derision from almost the second it was delivered. Instead of simply giving a speech, the president had decided to take a victory lap and landed in a jet on the aircraft carrier as if he was a professional wrestler making an entrance. This needless stunt was criticized heavily as being dangerous, expensive and ultimately unnecessary as Bush could have made the trip by helicopter. Still, if that excess had been the worst blunder of the day, nobody would remember the speech.

Instead, the event became a touchstone for Democrats and made the never-ending wars in Iraq and Afghanistan key points in the eventual political tide that would make it possible for a largely unknown African American Senator to take the White House, leading his party to sweeping gains in Congress. Of course, those gains would be lost two years later partially because like his predecessor who declared "mission accomplished," Barack Obama could not get American troops out of Iraq.

After this speech, which has been lampooned on every late-night show and by comics, radio hosts and anyone else who sees the absurdity of declaring an end to a war that still hadn't ended eight years later, Bush actually moved more troops in Iraq. Instead of accomplishing any sort of mission, Bush actually managed to make things worse in that the only thing propping up Iraqi society remains American troops. Without Saddam Hussein and his centralized evil, Iraq would quickly become a frontier of localized evil where petty dictators and warlords rule the day. If that was the goal, then, well, "mission accomplished," otherwise, some work remains to be done.

Stupid, Lying Politicians: Sometimes, You Just Have to Admit You Were Caught

Politicians, at least some of them, have no hesitations when it comes to lying to the American people. Usually, these lies are about what they plan to do in office, "I'm going to lower taxes," or "I will demand that the troops be brought home," and, though we may not believe them, there's no real way to prove that the person actually lied. Sometimes, though, a politician will get caught with his hand in the proverbial cookie jar (or perhaps with his pants around his ankles) and his instinct tells them to lie and everything will be better. This, of course, never works and has resulted in some of the more ridiculous political scandals of all time.

Perhaps the worst of these would be John Edwards blatantly lying to the public while running for president while his wife battled cancer. Before his scandal the public largely thought of Edwards as a prissy rich guy who got $200 haircuts before taking a limousine ride to his club. And, while Edwards had a reputation as an elitist, his wife Elizabeth was perceived as the ideal political wife. Pretty—at least for politics—Mrs. Edwards was the picture of a perfect parent, who supported her husband, had dinner on the table and a scotch on one those little serving trays ready when he walked through the door. She was well-liked by the American people largely because she stayed in the background and let her husband be the star. She was popular more because of what we didn't know about her than what we did, but she was popular nonetheless.

Under those circumstances that would make it a pretty bad idea for John to cheat on her in general. Throw in the fact that she was also dealing with terminal lung cancer and cheating on her becomes akin to

DANIEL B. KLINE AND JASON TOMASZEWSKI

drowning a sack of kittens in front of a group of little girls then shooting the girls for crying.

But, as foolish as John Edwards was for cheating on his wife, his true idiocy comes from the fact that he was having an affair and fathering a love child behind his cancer-stricken wife's back, while running for president. Short of being a performance artist who lives in a glass house, there is probably no more visible position than candidate for president. Not only are you watched by an enormous amount of media, you are also thoroughly investigated by your opponents. It's a bad idea to run for president while hiding an unpaid parking ticket, but doing it while trying to conceal marital infidelity is extremely foolish.

Of course, this has happened before, but when Gary Hart was caught cheating on his wife while not only running for president, but leading the race for his party's nomination, tabloid coverage of candidates barely existed. Now, with the Internet and the prevalence of cell phones, Hart would never have brazenly snuck off for some monkey business on the Monkey Business with Donna Rice. At least in Hart's case, we didn't know who his wife was so he was just a regular jerk guilty of infidelity.

Like Hart, when first confronted with evidence of his affair, Edwards lied. As rumors of a love child started swirling, Edwards continued to lie until basically the media trotted out the woman he had been cheating with (along with her child, who Edwards had, in fact, fathered). Edwards lied as long as it was possible, making him not only guilty of being a jerk, but being a special kind of lying jerk—one so arrogant and insensitive that he cheated on his wife and fathered a child with his mistress while his wife took care of the kids and tried not to die.

Also employing the Edwards deny and lie strategy was former South Carolina Governor Mark Sanford who we have to thank for forever making "hiking the Appalachian Trail" a euphemism for having an affair. On June 18 through June 24, 2009 Sanford, then still a sitting governor, simply disappeared. His wife had no idea where he was nor did the State Law Enforcement Division, which was essentially the Secret Service for South Carolina's governor. The governor did tell his staff he would be hiking on the Appalachian Trail, but concerns were raised when he did not answer 15 phone calls from his chief of staff and further alarms went up when he failed to call his family on Father's Day.

That might be because Sanford was not in fact hiking, he was instead spotted at an airport arriving on a flight from Argentina where he had been having an affair with a local woman. Instead of simply begging forgiveness, when Sanford ultimately confessed, he instead professed his love for that mistress.

As a Republican governor who preached the traditional right-wing, God and family agenda, Sanford might have been forgiven an extramarital affair. Had he come clean from the get go and both admitted his mistake and acted apologetic, he might have been able to dust himself off and live to fight another day. Instead, Sanford did the one thing you can't do when admitting to an affair and attempting to repair your image—he claimed to be in love. Once you use the "L" word, you can no longer claim you were tempted or that you made a mistake. Once you say "love," you're a scumbag who has no respect for your wife or the institution of marriage. That might be okay if you're a rock star or an actor, but most certainly not if you are a Republican governor.

Before South Carolina and the rest of the nation knew what a jerk Sanford was, we first had to wonder if he had died while hiking. As the story first broke, nobody considered that the governor was jetting off for a romantic getaway in Argentina, instead we were worried that he had gone hiking and had somehow become lost on the trail.

South Carolina's Lieutenant Govern Andre Bauer initially voiced concerns over Sanford's behavior and he publicly announced that announced that he could not "take lightly that his staff has not had communication with him for more than four days, and that no one, including his own family, knows his whereabouts."

Senate Minority Leader, Democrat John Land voiced the same concerns over Sanford's absence and openly questioned its timing. "It's one thing for the boys to go off by themselves," he said, "but on Father's Day to leave your family behind? That's erratic."

At this point though, people were either just worried about the governors safety or scoring political points from his apparent irresponsibility. Nobody considered that he might be part of an elaborate ruse to sneak away for a few days so he could cheat on his wife.

The concern over Sanford's whereabouts, however, led people to actually go looking for him. He might have actually gotten away it, but when he arrived back at Atlanta International Airport he was met by a single reporter, *The State's* Gina Smith who had received a tip that the governor was in Argentina. On a hunch, she guessed that he would have to fly back through Atlanta and her hunch turned out to break the whole story wide open as within a few hours, the governor held a press conference when he admitted that the hiking trip was a lie. He would also, in the next few days, call the woman he was cheating with his "soul mate," pretty much dooming his political career if his bizarre lies had not already done that.

Sanford also made the mistake of denying that he had used public funds to pay for his love trysts when it was later proven that he actually had. This led to an overall investigation of Sanford's use of public funds which revealed a variety of improprieties including the alleged use of a state planes to fly to get a haircut.

Somehow, though, Sanford did not resign from office, nor was he impeached. Because he was ineligible to run for reelection due to term limits and the fact that Bauer, the man who would replace him were he to step down or be forced out, was also a controversial figure, he was allowed to finish his term, which ended in January 2011.

AOL and Time Warner Merge: Making Way Less with More

Though it seems unfathomable in retrospect, America Online (AOL) once ruled the fledgling Internet world. The company which sold dial-up Internet service essentially was the Internet for nearly twenty million Americans. The company, which emerged as the winner over other early dial-up providers like CompuServe and Prodigy essentially had a license to print money. That said, that license clearly had an expiration date as either sooner or later, most of the country would move to broadband connection, making dial-up and AOL obsolete.

Unlike Yahoo!, Amazon.com, or Google, which would become better products as Americans got faster Internet access, AOL would literally become unnecessary. No more dial-up connection meant no more people paying $19.95 a month to AOL, not to mention no more captive audience to sell to advertisers.

No dummy, AOL's then CEO Steve Case knew he needed to become a content provider or somehow diversify his offering beyond dial-up Internet service. AOL may have been worth billions of dollars, but that valuation was tied to a core product rapidly approaching its expiration date.

Fortunately for AOL, Time Warner CEO Gerald Levin only noticed that AOL had twice Time Warner's valuation with less than half the cash flow. The Internet was the future, and pesky details like making money and a rapidly eroding core customer base would be problems that solve themselves through the magic of the stock market. When the merger happened, few if anyone, in the media questioned the deal even though Time Warner was essentially bringing in all the assets but would be the junior partner in the deal.

Originally valued at $350 billion, the merger quickly led to disaster as the two companies learned they were not as synergistic as they thought, and that simply buying an Internet company did not make your old-media products modern. Though it was originally hailed as being a landmark deal and widely praised, the bloom quickly fell off the rose, and only a few months after the merger, in May of 2000, signs of impending doom started to appear.

At first, it was simply a drop in online advertising—which was happening to everyone due to the dot-com bubble bursting. Then, AOL began losing subscribers at a growing rate, and the upcoming dominance of broadband Internet seemed obvious. It was also discovered during this time period that AOL had falsely inflated its advertising revenue (they ultimately paid a huge fine), which led to its high valuation in the first place. While this was happening, efforts to combine the two companies were not going well as they had decidedly different cultures.

As things continued to get worse, AOL/Time Warner shed value almost as fast as it shed employees. Ted Turner, who had sold his company to Time Warner previously, lost 80 percent of his net worth—approximately $8 billion—and countless others lost millions. This included many AOL paper millionaires—early employees who had stayed with the company, amassing stock options worth millions at one point. As the merged company's stock sank, many of these folks not only lost their jobs, they watched their nest eggs disappear.

The two companies stayed one until 2009, when Time Warner realized that it was better off not owning AOL than owning it. Of course, during that time, the environment changed again, and Time Warner's traditionally successful properties were battered by the sinking economy.

Once again an independent company, AOL has struggled to reinvent itself as a content provider. In 2010, the company launched hundreds of local news sites under the Patch banner, but so far, their efforts have been all money out and very little money in. Suffice to say, both companies and thousands of people were hurt by the ill-fated merger. Though values of course fluctuate, when the failure was finally admitted and the two companies separated, their combined worth was less than one-seventh of what it was when the merger occurred. It seems sometimes, one plus one actually equals zero.

ESPERANTO

Patro nia, kiu estas
en la cielo. Sanktig-
ata estu via nomo.
Venu via regno. Fa-
rigu via volo, ki-
el en la cielo, tiel
ankaŭ sur la tero.
Nian panon ĉiutag-
an donu al ni hod-
iaŭ. Kaj pardonu al
ni niajn ŝuldojn,
kiel ankaŭ ni pardo-
nas al niaj ŝuldantoj.
Kaj ne konduku nin en
tenton. Sed liberigu nin
de la malbono.
                    Amen.

Esperanto: The Language for Everyone as Used By No One

The idea of a universal language spoken by people all over the globe has been central to science fiction pretty much since that genre has existed. In the *Star Wars* universe, no matter what species a character was, they could at least understand "basic." Chewbacca may lack the vocal chord requirements to speak to Han Solo, but he could understand everything his human pal said because they shared this universal language.

In sci-fi, this convenient device made it easier for everyone to communicate without wasting pages or screen time coming up with devices that allow people to talk to each other. In the real world, a universal language would theoretically break down international borders, make it easier for the world's peoples to get along and generally make humanity more united.

The problem with creating a universal language, though, lies not so much in designing one (Dr. Ludovic Lazarus Zamenhof did that in the 1880s) but in getting people to actually be willing to learn it, speak it, and use it in everyday life. In design, Zamenhof's language, Esperanto, was everything it was supposed to be. A relatively easy-to-learn, politically neutral language that would allow people from different countries and cultures to communicate.

Unfortunately, more people speak Klingon—the language created for the bad guys on *Star Trek*—than actually speak Esperanto, and while the concept makes sense, the people of the world have largely rejected the concept. Realistically, much of the world has a problem getting its citizens to speak one language, let alone teaching their people a second one of dubious value. Even here in the United States, we still have plenty of high school graduates who don't read English very well, so it seems implausible to think we would be able to get the nation as a whole to take up speaking Esperanto.

Though Esperanto is spoken in over one hundred countries, estimates say that as few as ten thousand people to as many as two million people actively use the language. That's impressive for a language that has no native speakers, but it's still way less than the amount of people who watch an episode of the least popular prime time program on any given night. In fact, if that entire community of Esperanto speakers all watched the same show—and that number was on the high side of the estimate— that program would likely get cancelled were it airing on MTV.

Other Educational Failures

The metric system. Pretty much the entire world uses the metric system, but the United States has stubbornly refused to adopt it. It's not that we haven't tried—huge efforts were made in the 1970s and 1980s to teach it in schools—but Americans seem unwilling to drop our confusing system for the much more logical metric system. In the system used in the United States, we have oddities like twelve inches in a foot. The metric system does everything in multiples of ten, but something that simple and logical simply does not fly here.

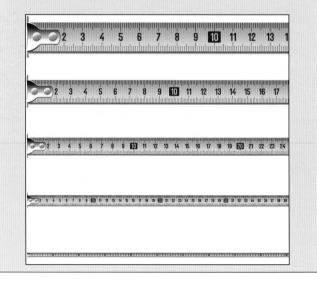

Teaching Latin. Despite the fact that nobody actually speaks Latin, U.S. schools continue to teach it with the logic that studying Latin provides a good base for learning other languages. Of course, you could just spend that time learning the other language rather than studying one that's only useful to know which Super Bowl you are watching.

The new math. In the 1960s, largely driven by America's fear that the Soviets were ahead of us in science because Sputnik was launched before we had a space vessel, new math was foisted upon America's schoolchildren. This concept, which was widely disliked by parents, did not catch on largely because the system was so different than what had previously been taught that parents could not help their kids with their homework. After a very brief attempt at making new math the national standard, the program was dropped. Ultimately, the perceived edge in math and science that the Soviet Union had did not result in them beating the United States at much of anything.

The Reebok Debacle: Dan O'Brien and Dave Johnson's Olympic Ads

During the buildup to the 1992 Summer Olympics in Barcelona, Reebok decided to build its Olympic ad campaign around America's two decathlon gold medal hopefuls, Dan O'Brien and Dave Johnson. This hugely expensive campaign kicked off with ads featuring "Dan and Dave" running during Super Bowl XXVI.

Initially, the ads were a huge success, turning both O'Brien and Johnson—who were complete unknowns because, well, decathletes don't usually get a lot of mainstream publicity and major companies most certainly do not build gigantic ad campaigns around them. The commercials were a bit of a last-ditch effort by Reebok, which had been losing market share to Nike to regain its place at the top of the U.S. sneaker market.

The commercials, which aired in heavy rotation, were built around the theme, "Who will be the world's greatest athlete—Dan or Dave? To be settled in Barcelona."

Unfortunately, likely due to the added scrutiny, pressure and demands on his time placed by being a media star, O'Brien failed to qualify for the Olympics as he botched his pole vault during the Olympic trials in New Orleans. In pole vaulting, contestants have the right to not jump until the competition reaches a height they consider worthy of their ability. In doing so, the competitors save energy and avoid making a lot of jumps at heights they can easily clear. On the other hand, they also run the risk of not clearing any height and receiving no points for the event. That is what happened to O'Brien who went from being a gold medal contender to watching the Olympics on television.

Reebok attempted to salvage the spots by modifying them to have Dan cheering Dave on in his quest for the gold medal. That quest failed too as Dave managed only a bronze in Barcelona. So in the battle of Dan versus Dave to see who the best athlete in the world was, the answer was Robert Zmeick of the Czech Republic.

Prohibition: The "Noble Experiment" Goes Horribly Wrong

In the 1920s many Americans pretended they were in favor of banning all sales, manufacturing and consumption of alcohol. Unfortunately, saying you were against drinking and not actually liking drinking did not go hand in hand. Much in the way that most people now claim to not buy any porn, yet porn is a multi-billion dollar industry, alcohol in the early part of the 1900s had the same stigma. Everyone pretended to be above having a few shots of whiskey or a couple of beers, but when the doors were closed, plenty of people enjoyed the hard stuff.

DANIEL B. KLINE AND JASON TOMASZEWSKI

Because alcohol consumption was not socially acceptable—largely due to the religious beliefs of the time—the public stood idly by while an actual amendment was added to the Constitution. The vast majority of the public did not support prohibition, but nobody was willing to stand up and admit that they enjoyed drinking and did not think it should be outlawed.

Lasting from 1920 to 1933, Prohibition did eliminate the legal production of alcohol. It also created a huge industry involved in the illegal production of alcohol and led to the creation of thousands of "speakeasies." These establishments pretended they were merely social clubs serving legal beverages, but everyone knew that they actually served alcohol. Much like the Chinese restaurants in the 1980s that would allegedly serve beer to underage patrons if they ordered the "cold tea," the speakeasies worked using thinly veiled codes.

Prohibition was only loosely enforced and the public became disenchanted with the law during the Great Depression when people had more than a few reasons to want a drink. With the law mostly only working to create a gigantic criminal underground (which had replaced the once successful legal manufacturers of alcohol) and causing enormous problems for police, Prohibition was ultimately repealed in 1933—making it the only Constitutional amendment to ever be reversed.

Though Prohibition was unsuccessful, it did succeed in devastating the city of St. Louis, which had been one of the major producers of beer for the nation. This contributed to the

already rampant unemployment that occurred during the Great Depression. The law also helped fuel the growth of the Mafia in the United States as the criminal organization controlled much of the flow of illegal liquor. This led to U.S. cities becoming battlegrounds between rival gangs—turning once safe streets into dangerous war-zones. Crime increased in major cities across the country by over 20% and drug addiction (because drunks couldn't get a drink when they wanted it) rose by more than 40%. In some cases, desperate for a fix, alcoholics would turn to drinking Sterno, a substance that did mimic the effects of alcohol while poisoning and sometimes killing the person who merely wanted a drink.

Celebrity Baby Names: Facebook, Apple and Banjo are Not Names

Celebrities—by the general nature of being famous—are used to standing out and being in the public eye. Because of that, they forget that not everyone wants attention called to themselves and there actually are people—even children of famous people—who prefer a more anonymous lifestyle. For a lot of celebrities, though, the idea that their kids would not also be famous seems impossible so in naming their kids, they choose names that are guaranteed to stand out. They do this without any regard for the fact that their kids already have to grow up with famous parents and that perhaps the added burden of being named after Superman's Kryptonian name (Nicholas Cage's son Kal-El), an inanimate object (Rachel Griffiths' son Banjo) or just being given a plain old ridiculous moniker (Penn Jillette's daughter Moxie CrimeFighter) might make a difficult life even harder.

Since many celebrities seem unwilling to give their children the option of having a normal life, we are instead left with kids who must bear names that invite mocking and require explanation for the rest of their lives. These kids not only have to spend their lives being judged by the accomplishments of their parents, they must also do so with names that only make sense if you are famous. It's hard to introduce yourself as "Moon Unit," without also explaining that your dad was Frank Zappa and, well, that pretty much sets the tone for your entire life.

Though the list of horrifyingly bad names famous people have saddled their kids with is extensive, here are some of the worst:

True Harlow (Joely Fisher's daughter)

Diva Muffin (Another Frank Zappa daughter)

Indiana August (Casey Affleck and Summer Phoenix' daughter)

Pilot Inspektor (Jason Lee's son)

Poet Sienna Rose (Soleil "Punky Brewster" Moon Frye's daughter)

Seven Sirius (Erykah Badu's son)

Apple (Gwyneth Paltrow and Chris Martin's daughter)

Bronx Mowgli (Ashley Simpson and Pete Wentz' son)

Petal Rainbow Blossom and her sister Poppy Honey (daughters of chef Jamie Oliver)

Of course, giving your kids horrible names is not solely the purview of celebrities as one lucky Egyptian boy—after the country's revolt that ousted the nation's long-time dictator—has been saddled with the name Facebook. At least he isn't MySpace or Friendster, but living in Egypt with the first name Facebook takes what will likely be a difficult life and make it worse.

Acknowledgements

This book—at least our second attempt at getting this book published—started with a bad idea.

It started when Dan, standing alone at Boston's Paradise Rock Club watched Buffalo Tom—his long-time favorite band—get up on stage in front of a sold-out crowd where they played new songs that held the audience as much as their familiar classics (well, classics to those of us who have had the joy of knowing who Buffalo Tom are). On that night, though he was happily employed, running a very cool toy store for really good money for a boss who treated him like family (and yes, that is meant as a positive), Dan decided to quit his job.

In a time where jobs were scarce and countless people we knew had been unemployed for over a year, Dan walked away from in the neighborhood of six figures without a backup plan beyond a vague plan to sell this book—something that if we managed to beat the very long odds to accomplish would bring us at most the equivalent of a few week's salary, which we would then have to split.

That was a foolish plan and a classic bad idea, but we didn't have a better one.

And while selling this book and having it actually get released was a bit of a dream come true, it did not (as of this writing) put much money into our bank accounts. Had the story ended with the book coming out, both my writing partner Jason and I would be very available for book signings as we lived out of our cars eating nothing but press releases and publisher's proofs.

My bad idea, however, either through inspiration or blind luck has led to both of us stumbling into new lives where we never would have gone were it not for that Buffalo Tom concert and a proposal so old that people still used their cell phones mostly to make phone calls when we wrote it.

During this time, Jason was laid off from his job working at my family's business. One would not think I would have to worry about my family laying off one of my closest friends (who did a good job) but one would be wrong, and much like me, Jason was out of work—though much less happily. And while we were grappling with unemployment and dreams of publishing stardom, my wife, Celine, who had been very supportive of my foolish choice to become voluntarily unemployed during the worst economy of our lifetimes, was also struggling at her job and looking to move on.

At this point, the story could go horribly off course as it does for nearly every person behind every bad idea in this book. In my case, however, my bad idea turned into a consulting gig with a website for teachers where the general manager asked me to evaluate their operation. This turned into me overseeing a revamp of their website—a project which Jason helped me on and which Celine offered her insights on as well. And when the time came to relaunch the site with a new team behind it, well, Jason started a few weeks early as associate editor before Celine joined him as editor.

So with that backdrop, it's important to say that this book would not be possible without the support of Steve Maynard, formerly my employer and forever my friend. In addition, Steve's wife Pam has been strongly in my corner as have his two oldest sons, Alex and Patrick, as well as the rest of the Time Machine Family. Thanks also go to Rich Datz at EducationWorld.com for inadvertently providing Jason and Celine with a lifeline.

Dan would also like to thank his brother Todd, as the past few years would have been impossible without him. Dan also thanks his long-time friends, Allison Atkins, Ellen Maccarone, and Lauren Moynihan as well as their families for the support they have always provided. Also, as this book was conceived, written, and ultimately sold, both Jeff Colchamiro and Jennifer Barrows Fox lived through the highs and the lows with us and their support kept me going more than a few times.

And of course, Dan wishes to thank Buffalo Tom, for showing him that even if you couldn't conquer the world, you could still move forward as an artist.

Jason would like to thank his father Robert for all of the worst ideas he proposed that didn't make the final cut. He would also like to thank Mark Tomaszewski for always supporting his writing career and for giving him brutally honest advice. Finally, Jason would like to thank everyone who ever listened to the *Worst of the Week* podcast; you guys are the ones that keep the bad ideas flowing.

We also could not have done this without our wives, Celine Provini and Dawn Tomaszewski, who put up with our endless phone calls, weekends spent working on our podcast, and everything else we put them through in the interest of humor. The same could be said of our former Lynn Ladder co-workers, specifically Frank Koughan, Duane Boucher, Steve Young, and Mark Krook as well as our entire crew in New Haven. We truly appreciate the support.

Last, we wish to thank our editor, Ann Treistman, who told us the book was funny and didn't make us change our vision.

Other publishing companies offered us more money. Nobody else offered us a place that actually believed in us.

Find more bad ideas and our weekly podcast at WorstIdeas-Ever.com.